FORE

John McClain is a Houston legend who has been a writer at the Houston Chronicle for over 40 years.

When Fred Faour disclosed to me his idea of writing a script based on Jesus returning as a gambler in Chicago, we were on a golf course, and I believe I was lining up a putt. He swore he didn't do it to distract me so he could win a few bucks.

At the time, Fred was the assistant sports editor at the Houston Chronicle and one of my bosses. We had been good friends for years, and we were known to have exchanged some hard-earned dollars on golf courses around Houston. I had known him since he was a child because his father - "Big Fred" was one of my mentors at the Chronicle and the best copy editor, headline writer and layout specialist I ever had the honor of working under.

So "Little Fred" knew I wouldn't be too upset if his idea about Jesus caused me to think just enough to miss the putt, which I did. Later, on the 19th hole, we downed a couple of beers, and I had to admit I was intrigued about his idea. Skeptical? Of course. Interested? Heck yeah.

I mean, if Jesus can be born in a manger, grow up as a carpenter in Nazareth and preach the gospel to thousands of loyal followers as he travels through the countryside, why couldn't he return as a biker/

gambler in Chicago who makes his way to Houston winning bets and piling up money at racetracks and in casinos?

The evolution of Fred's original idea is fascinating. From a script to a book to a script and, finally, to this inspiring, character-driven, captivating story built around Jesse Christian and his rogue's gallery of disciples – Louis, Michael, Mare and Sophie – each of whom make Jesus Just Left Chicago one wild ride.

As I watched Fred be promoted to sports editor of the Houston

Chronicle and later become a college teacher and now a popular, highly rated sports talk show host, I was always impressed that he never allowed his day job to interfere with his determination to bring his unique idea about Jesus to the public.

I've been working in the Houston Chronicle sports department for 44 years, covering the National Football League, including the Houston Oilers and Houston Texans, since 1977. I'm an avid reader of fiction because it gives me a way to separate from football when I want to kick back and relax. I have to admit how excited I have been to get my copy of Jesus Just Left Chicago.

Fred's always been a gambler at heart – in life as well as at the racetrack and poker tables. As he updated me about his project through the years, I became more and more interested. I've eagerly awaited publication because I know how much this labor of love has meant to him and how much imagination he's put into the finished product.

I'm not surprised Fred has been able to follow through on his idea and develop Jesus Just Left Chicago for what should be an international audience. Even though he was an editor – meticulous just like his father – he was also a terrific writer, as you'll see in his novel. Knowing how much of himself he put into Jesus Just Left Chicago makes me even more impressed with the whirlwind of experiences we share with Jesse and his friends as they move from racetracks, to casinos to seedy gambling parlors across the country.

Just who is Jesse Christian? Is he The Messiah? Are his followers disciples? Delve into this enthralling character who's the brainchild of Fred Faour and decide for yourself. Jesus Just Left Chicago – you won't be able to put it down!

- John McClain

JESUS JUST LEFT CHICAGO

A Novel

By

Fred Faour

BOOK ONE: THE GOSPEL ACCORDING TO LOUIS CHAPTER ONE

My name is Louis. I killed Jesus. I have been trying to live with that. I can't anymore. How do you live with killing Jesus? How do you live with the greatest crime in history? There's no redemption for that. No forgiveness. Not from anyone. You must think I'm crazy. I'm not crazy. I am a little drunk. I've been trying to think of a way to deal with this, to come to grips with the greatest sin ever. Get it out of my head.

This is what I have come up with: tell you the story. Get it all out there. Confess to you. Tell you why. Maybe you will believe me, maybe you won't. One thing is for sure: I believe. I met Jesus. I was his friend. And I betrayed him. I killed him.

There's no real way to deal with that. Not much precedent. Tried to call Judas a few times and figure out what he did, but they don't have a hotline to hell. Guess I will see him soon enough, though. That will be a lonely spot at the bar in hell – Judas and me. I'm not there yet. Just in case, I bought a fifth of Jack Daniels. Black label, the good stuff. Don't plan on taking any of it with me, though. Just thought I would start working on the bottle and writing my story. More than a story, really. The longest suicide note in history.

My plan is pretty simple. When I get to the bottom of this bottle, I hope to have told you everything I know. And I hope someone will believe me. And then I am going to take this beautiful piece of cold, hard steel – a .45 my dad gave me a long time ago, with his initials carved in tiny letters on the trigger -- and blow my brains all over this computer. I wonder what that will look like. Will it spray? Will it splatter? Will it be black? Red? Will it clot? Will I see pieces of my own brain before I die? I wonder how many seconds I will have before it all goes dark. Before I go to hell. I wonder if the bullet will go through my brain and destroy the computer. Wouldn't that suck? My suicide note ruined in the blast? Wouldn't that be ironic? Hell, maybe no one ever sees it. That would be the greatest sin of all.

I'm going to write it anyway. Maybe my kids will get to see it. (I wonder how they will handle being the children of the most evil man ever? They will keep some therapists in business for a long ass time!) Maybe my ex-wives. They won't be surprised, that's for sure. Oh well. I am writing it for whoever reads it. But mostly I am writing it for me. That's all I ever really wanted to do anyway -- write. Like everything else, I was just never very good at it. At least not until Jesse showed up. Everything got better when Jesse Christian was around. (Sorry, Jesse was Jesus. I'll get to that. Weak attempt to get you to keep reading. There's some technique there, but I don't remember what it's called). I'm a little drunk. Did I mention that? I had a few beers before I started this Jack. I don't usually drink beer. Always Jack. Jack and Coke. Turned Jesse onto it for a while, but he always went back to wine. Man, there's something about Jack and Coke… smooth, a little sweet, a nice punch. Gets you there pretty quickly.

Five or six really strong ones and you are good for the night.

I don't have any Coke, though. Today, it's straight Jack. Except for the last little bit. I do have a Diet Coke, and I will mix it with that. Won't be the same, but then I expect to be too drunk to care at that point. Just want my last drink to be Jack and Coke. Or close enough. You probably think it should be red wine. No way I ever drink that again. Not after what I did. At least I have that glow. That warm, just-a-little-drunk glow. It's all I have. And thanks to it, I can be honest with you. Of course, it's probably why I failed so much as a writer. Probably stayed drunk too much.

I have no idea how I became the most evil person in history. I mean, Hitler looks like a choir boy next to me. Wow. That's a tough one to figure out. I was a good kid. Hell, I was an altar boy. Snuck a little wine every now and then, but who didn't? I had good parents. My dad worked in the refineries. Got cancer from whatever stuff he inhaled every day and died at 50. My mom stayed at home and raised all of us. She wanted to be a romance novelist. I guess that's where my interest in writing came from. She sucked at it, too. And I don't think they had much of a romance.

There was a neighbor who visited a lot. She only seemed happy around him. I figured out later they had been carrying on for years. Apparently he wasn't her only beau, either. Guess I inherited her curse. I was always more like her, and I hated that. But I didn't want to work in the refineries, either. I went to junior college, took writing classes, met a girl, got married, got a divorce. Wrote short stories for a while, then tried writing technical journals. Then I worked as a reporter. Covered all kinds of stuff for the local newspaper.

I wasn't very good at any of it. Stayed drunk too much. I think I mentioned that. But I enjoyed reporting. My favorite was the cop beat. That's where you stayed at the police station, and went to cover stories when something weird happened. I saw a lot of cool stuff – double homicides, drug-related murders…all kinds of bloody stuff. Galveston had some bad people back then. Oh yeah, forgot to mention: I grew up in Galveston. That's where I am now. Galveston is a failed port on the Texas coast. A nothing little island that's a lot like New Orleans without the tourists or the French Quarter. (New Orleans is where I killed Jesus, by the way. We will get to that).

Saw a lot of cool stuff in Galveston, mostly when I covered cops. Man, that beat was fun. One time I went with the police to an auto-pedestrian accident. The victim's body was twisted under the tire base of an 18-wheeler, but he was still alive when we got there. He was breathing fast, blood everywhere, his body broken in all different ways. I wondered why he wouldn't die. He just kept whispering, "forgive me. Forgive me." I know it's sick, but I laughed. "You are asking the wrong guy, chief." He kept begging anyway. Right before he died, one of his eyes actually blew out of his head. He had some weird hemorrhage in his brain. Essentially, his eye exploded. He didn't die right away, even then. He reached up with the one arm that was only partially broken and tried to put his eye back. I admired that. So did the paramedics. They gave him a shot of morphine as a reward. He had no chance, and they knew it. They could never have gotten his body out of the wheel base, even if he'd had a chance. It took them hours even after he died.

I watched him die that night, just after midnight, a man I would never know. He was just road kill to me. But he wound up making an impact, because that night I decided I was truly sick. I enjoyed watching him die. My story in the paper the next day didn't really do it justice. It read like this:

"GALVESTON – A Texas City man was killed when he was struck by a tractor-trailer truck Monday night at Highway 45 and 61st street.

John Economy, 27, was attempting to cross highway 45 on foot at night when he was struck by the vehicle.

He died at the scene.

Economy was unemployed and had no known address and no known living relatives. He graduated from Texas City High School in 1983 as class Valedictorian.

Services are pending."

I always wondered about John Economy. How he went from being the smartest kid in school to a guy who got killed crossing a freeway in the middle of the night. A guy who died begging for forgiveness, wrapped around the wheelbase of a Nabisco truck, his eye blown all over the pavement. I also wondered why I wrote such lousy news stories. I tried sports for a while, then features. Then I tried teaching. Then I met another woman, had another wife. Three kids. Another divorce, too. My fault this time. The curse of my mother.

10

It occurred to me for no real reason that had John Economy lived, we would be the same age. We'd both be 43. I think John got it right. He checked out before he fucked up his life. I waited too long. I should have gone a long time ago. I think that's what a truly smart, sick person realizes: you can't escape the sickness. Mine was drinking and gambling. And I couldn't get away from it. Most people with my sickness just go broke. I wound up killing Jesus. Damn. This Jack tastes good. I hope they have it in hell. I wish you could see this view. A little alcohol glaze really makes it beautiful. I bought a little condo on Galveston Bay. Summer is coming. It's unseasonably cool, and the sun is setting on the water. I doubt I will see the sunrise. I hope to be done before then.

Something you should know about Galveston Bay: it's dirty. It's brown. You can't see your feet when you walk in the water. But when the sun sets, it makes the ugly brown glimmer and shine. It gives it an odd, white-ish hue that looks almost like ice. Today, the horizon is framed with a huge thunderstorm just off the coast. The sun is behind the top of the huge, cumulus clouds, spreading a weird, orange color across the sky. It looks like someone set off an A-bomb, and the explosion stopped halfway through and froze itself in the sky.

I came here because every important decision I made was done staring out over Galveston Bay or the Gulf of Mexico. Over this water, I decided to try to be a writer. I decided to get married. Twice. And divorced. Twice. And I decided to kill Jesse Christian. Turned out he was Jesus. Damn. Blew that one, huh? There is a comfort in this water. My life has been built around it. I've lived most of it here. Now I am going to die

11

here. My name is Louis. I killed Jesus. I told you that already, didn't I? Sorry, I'm a little drunk. Guess I better tell you how I killed him.

BOOK TWO: THE GOSPEL ACCORDING TO LOUIS CHAPTER TWO

The water is warm as it washes over me. I close my eyes, and imagine the crimson mixing with the slightly grey bath water. Slowly at first, the blood crawls alongside me. It looks like flowers. Growing crimson flowers. Funny, I thought when the water was warm, you weren't supposed to feel the pain. My wrists hurt where I cut the arteries. The flowers are bigger now. Bigger still. The tub is red. Damn, suddenly it's cold. I was supposed to be warm. Going to close my eyes for the last time now. The pain will go away forever. The water starts spilling onto the floor.

"Shit!"

I quickly turned off the faucet. Fell asleep in the tub again. Can't tell you how many times I have had that fantasy. Oh well. Just dreaming. When I really kill myself, it will be much more obvious. Louder. I am going out with a bang. I had that dream the day I met Jesse Christian. He was so easy to notice. He had a presence about him, a glow. Something that made him stand out. We've all seen people like that. People we want to be around. People who have that glow about them.

We were at our table that day. Some of us, anyway. The tellers at the race track called us The Dirty Dozen, because there were twelve of us who went to the track almost every day. We lived there. It was our home.

Our table. Our place. No one other than the twelve sat at that table. If one of us was there, and a friend who wasn't one of the twelve showed up, then they weren't allowed to sit there. It was our own private little corner of the world.

We used to be thirteen, but Fat Johnny had a stroke. Johnny was an oil executive. A lot of those in Houston. Lived life hard and fast. Enjoyed every second. Enjoyed it too much. The day he had his stroke, he was sitting at the table. He could hardly talk. He would have cried for help if he could have. No one noticed. They were so caught up in the drinking and gambling…hell, we all were. We didn't notice when he staggered to his feet and somehow made it to his car. We found out the next day that's where he died. No one went to the funeral. Johnny showered his friends with cash, alcohol, whatever they needed. But when he crashed, there was no one there to help. Not me, not any of us.

Jesse showed up after that. If he had come sooner, maybe things would have been different. Maybe, but I don't know. Jesse taught us to care. Damn Jesse. Drove up on a big black Harley, covered in leather. I thought it was funny that he parked the bike just outside the pavilion instead of in the parking lot. Yet no one complained. It was a winter day, perfect weather. Not a speck of a cloud in the sky. One of those days where the only white you saw was the vapor trails when jets flew over. We didn't really have winter in Houston, so if you are from up north, you would laugh at me calling it that. It was about 45 degrees. What you guys might call autumn weather.

He was all dressed in black leather, dark sunglasses, long, curly flowing hair, perfectly crafted beard. If Michael Madsen had gone to a Halloween party dressed as a Jesus biker…well, that was Jesse. We didn't notice much at the track. You probably figured that out from the Fat Johnny story. But we noticed Jesse. Noticed him when he sat at the table next to us. When such a big, impressive guy ordered a wimpy drink like red wine. When none of us said anything about how this was a private table, and we did not allow people we did not know. What we really noticed was he kept bringing back winning tickets. Everyone notices that. And when he won at least six races in a row… well, that makes you an instant superstar with the DDs. We also noticed the angel tattoo on his left arm, with one word: "dad." But we didn't care about that. Just the winning.

I was the first to talk to him. Didn't take long for me to go over there, because I was losing. I was strangely drawn to him, mostly because of his routine. Handicap race. Buy ticket. Cash ticket. Wash, rinse, repeat. "Hey dude," I said. I was great at saying "dude." Called everybody that in one way or another. Girls loved it. But you have to know how to use it, or you sound like an idiot. My ex could never say it right, never make it work. She was an idiot, though. But I was an expert at using the word "dude." However, I was impressed immediately, because Jesse was better. "Dude, have a seat," he said.

Just like that. And I did. At his command, like he was some young hottie I had been working all night and she had suddenly said yes. So I moved from my usual seat, the place I had been at every day for almost

15

four years, and sat at the other end of the table, next to Jesse. In Fat Johnny's old seat. We talked about nothing, but we hit it off. It was like he knew everything about me, all my failures, all my dreams. And he knew I was curious about his winning. At the same time, he was comfortable with me. He felt like a friend I had known forever. Maybe one who didn't like me -- most of the DDs were like that when it came to me -- but a friend nonetheless. He stared at me with piercing blue eyes that seemed to tell me I was the failure I thought I was. But somehow, around him, it was OK. I was OK. He didn't care that I was a failure. He seemed to expect it. Embrace it. When I finally asked what I wanted to, he already knew what I was after.

"What horse do you like the in the next race at Aqueduct?" Sam Houston had simulcasts from every track in the entire world, it seemed. You could bet on 200 races if you wanted to. We were all degenerates. We wanted to bet them all. We would find our tips anywhere, but usually we trusted the Dirty Dozen. We would pool bets, everyone throwing in a horse. Sometimes we won. More often than not, we didn't.

I mean, all of the DDs hit something sometimes. We had an unwritten rule at the table – whoever won big bought the drinks. That way, everyone got drunk. But if someone around us was on a hot streak…of course we would listen. "The 8 horse," he said. God, he had a great voice. Sounded like a radio star. And he was just a biker. The 8 horse was 25-1, a sick longshot. I was dubious. "What about the 1?" I asked. He was the even money favorite and looked like a lock. "Crippled," he said. "Bet the 8."

And on a leap of faith, I did. That was my first winner, courtesy of Jesse Christian. First of many. Then again, if you were Jesus, wouldn't you know who won every race? Oh yeah, we have a long way to go before that. But I became believer right then. At least in his handicapping skills. Anyone that makes me money...

I cashed for almost $800. Bought drinks. Invited Jesse to stay at the table. He cashed every race after that. Most of the rest of the DDs showed up later that day, and for once we all left with money. And happy. And we had a new person at the table, someone to replace Fat Johnny. We had Jesse. I had always been the table leader. The best handicapper. The smartest guy. On this day, I was happy to cede that title to Jesse. Let him be the man.

But I admit, I was a little jealous. I guess I never got over it. I wasn't a bad guy. I just liked being the center of attention. Sometimes I wonder if I ever grew up. There were times I was as emotional as a teen-ager. I would go from being charming, funny, smart, to drunk, petulant and jealous. That jealousy would come back to get us all.

BOOK THREE: THE GOSPEL ACCORDING TO MICHAEL CHAPTER ONE

I'm Michael. I'm damned. No one could save me. Not even Jesse. Nobody at the table knew what I really did. They suspected I was outfit. An Italian in the vending business – what else could I be? Most of them thought it was romantic, cool. I didn't do much to change their opinion. They had no real idea, however, what it was really like. What I really did. It wasn't something I liked to share. Only with my priest.

Oh yeah, the priest. I always wondered if it was my fault he strayed. If my stories didn't send him over the edge. If that's why he was caught with that little boy. After he was found out, I thought that maybe he secretly enjoyed hearing my stories. "Go on," he would say. I would give every detail. I wonder now, if he wasn't masturbating behind that wall. Dreaming he was watching me. I also wonder who was the sicker of the two of us.

It was the details he seemed to want. I gave them all. Only to him. God had already seen. Thirty times. Thirty souls I sent on their way, including the priest. That's why I believe in God. That's why I know I'm damned. I always felt them leave. The last few, I would try to get close, so I could feel the spirit leave their body; feel them go cold. It was mystical -- a religious experience. I think I have been closer to God than anyone. I sent people on to the next life.

I was a hit man. Not sure I mentioned that. Louis asked me to tell this story. I told him only after I was gone. I'm too old for jail. Louis was a hard guy to like -- he was so emotional. One day he was the happiest guy in the world, the next he would sulk like a depressed actor. Still, he was my friend. This is a pretty big leap of faith, trusting him with this. There was something about killing…it was orgasmic. That's why I suspect the priest was jacking off to my stories. He understood. He, too, was close to God.

It got easier each time. The first time, I was scared. It was hard to pull the trigger. I hesitated. I didn't want to be close. I felt nervous, and wasn't sure I could go through with it. But as soon as I held the . 22 in my hand, I knew I had found my purpose. What I was supposed to be. The Transition Man. The Angel of Vengeance. I looked my dad straight in the eye and put two in his forehead. The .22 wasn't powerful; the bullets lodged in his brain. He didn't die right away. In the movies, they always died fast. He staggered around, grabbed his head, kept trying to reach for invisible people who weren't there. He screamed like a little girl. He cursed me.

Then he thanked me, and I felt him leave. You'd be surprised how many thanked me. They were all screwed up souls who went astray somewhere. Somehow, they made the wrong enemy. My dad robbed from the family. He had to go. I didn't question it. He knew the day he did it he was going to die. Father John didn't thank me. He had to know what was coming. He was the last one I did – went into semi-retirement after that. The little boy was the son of a boss. The kid was never the same.

I am not a good man. I mentioned that. But priests who abused kids...who used their status to take advantage of the innocent...I don't think we will be in the same level in hell. At least I hope not. I might have enjoyed that one the most. I did it slow, cool. I made him beg. He stared up with cold, bleak, hopeless eyes. He never asked for forgiveness. He just asked to live. He died slowly. I cut out his tongue first. He still screamed, but it was grotesque, like a deaf person yelling, inaudible.

I assumed he kept it up the whole time, but I barely heard it. I had my headphones on, playing music. I always listened to music when I killed. Something about the sound...it made me see everything much more clearly. For Father John, I listened to "Sabbath Bloody Sabbath." Over and over again. Ozzie's piercing wail made a perfect companion as I cut little slices of flesh from the body, no more than an inch at a time. Then I would heat the big, cool Bowie knife and cauterize the wound. It took hours for him to die, a quivering, unrecognizable lump of flesh that fought death hard. I must have heard that song 200 times before he finally gave in.

Right before he died, I took off my headphones. His was a soft moan at that point, life barely left in him. I knew he didn't want to face what was next. I whispered some lines from the song.

"*Dreams turn to nightmares*

Heaven turns to hell

Burned out confusion

Nothing more to tell."

I smiled as he died, felt his dark soul move on to its next destination. I felt the cool tingle surrounding me, then the inevitable orgasm. It happened every time. I always had to wear a condom. I learned that the first time. That picture remains in my head even today; a dark, crimson lump of flesh, like an unclean side of beef hanging in a freezer. I was doing God's work that day, more than Father John ever did. I knew it was what He wanted. But I knew, too, I was damned for doing it. Kind of sucks that evil has to kill evil. The good could not do it. Hell, the good were afraid to even call the cops. It fell to a man like me. A damned man to kill the damned. So the priest would be my last victim, at least for a while. I would be my 31st. But not yet. So many songs in my head. The sweet irony of "Murder by Numbers." And one that would haunt me for a long time: "Ruby Tuesday."

She was my 23rd. A dazzling young blonde, full of life. Just a kid who loved the clubs and showing off how lyrically beautiful she was. A self-proclaimed gold-digger, she had hooked up with the wrong guy. Danny was an underboss, and a vicious, mean, perverted piece of flesh in an expensive suit. One day, drunk and high, 23 threatened to call the cops on him, and tell anyone who would listen about their relationship. I was the one who got the other call.

Danny was a married man. But then there's a great line in the movie Billy Bathgate. "We are all married men." I was a big movie buff.

Especially mob movies. But doing my job was never like it looked on film. I would stalk my prey for days sometimes, learning their routines. When they took their kids to school. Where they bought their coffee. What clubs they went to at night. The gyms they would go to during the day. I would study their co-workers. When it was time, I knew everything about them and everyone they knew. In fact, by the time I paid them a visit, I knew them better than the people who wanted them dead.

In 23's case, she loved to have fun. The daughter of a hairdresser and a guy who had picked up her mother in a bar and never been heard from again. She grew up with almost nothing, and quickly realized her looks were the key to being somebody. And boy did she use them. A rock star fell for her once. A baseball player. They showered her with gifts and money. And then they would always go back to their wives. Just like Danny. But Danny didn't leave any messes behind. Those were for me to clean up.

I never left any traces that it was a hit. In her case there was lots of jewelry that she was more than happy to flaunt. And drugs and cash. All easy to throw in a bag and make it look like a robbery. She was asleep, naked under her covers, a tanned, flawless leg hanging out once side when I slipped into her bedroom. As the female body goes, she was as perfect as you will find. She had been out drinking all night, and would not ever know what happened. She had just quietly passed out and would never wake up. I was OK with that. She was just a kid who got tied up with the wrong person. She wasn't like the priest. She wasn't someone who deserved it. She just stepped in the wrong pile of shit. I put on my headphones, and began playing Ruby Tuesday.

I shot her three times, suppressor keeping the neighbors from hearing anything. There was more blood than usual, and a tuft of fur exploded in the air. I thought it might be a pillow between her legs, but when I peeled the cover back, I saw what was left of a small, Siamese cat. It had been curled up between her legs, a hidden lump. Its blood mingled with the girl's, painting the sheets two hues of ugly crimson.

"Goodbye, Ruby Tuesday.

Who could hang a name on you?"

I put all the valuables in my bag and left, the song immediately taunting me. I had no problem killing at that point. I enjoyed it. But the cat? A helpless animal just trying to comfort its owner? That one haunted me. It haunts me still. Kind of silly, right? A guy who has sent 30 souls to the next world. That damned cat sticks with me. Fucking thing would still be alive if it had not crawled under the covers. And with all my studying, how the hell did I miss the cat? Not my best moment. That one felt like a sin. Yeah, I know. Mr. Killer thinks shooting a cat was a sin but popping the girl was OK. But the day I took out the priest helped wash away some of those sins. And the monetary payoff was more than enough to retire.

So I took my cash, moved to Houston and spent my days at the racetrack, with a lot of other lost souls. I ran my little vending business, but I never did any work. It was a reward from the boss for time served.

His crew did everything. I just collected a check and woke up each day wondering if this was the time I became No. 31. If I would put a bullet in my head while listening to music. I had no idea what song just yet. But each day, I had something to look forward to; a day at the races with people just as messed up as me. And each day, 31 seemed to fade a little farther into the future.

We were a weird mix at the track. It made sense that Jesse found us, me most of all. The others all had their dark flaws, too, but none like me. And all of them were like family in a sick, sadistic way. We were all connected. We were all beyond redemption. And deep down, that's all any of us ever wanted -- redemption. Jesse made us believe it was possible for a while. Even me. But I knew better. For all I had done, "Ruby Tuesday…" when I heard that song, I always felt chills when it played. No redemption there. None anywhere. But enough about me. You need to meet the rest of the table.

BOOK FOUR: THE GOSPEL ACCORDING TO MICHAEL CHAPTER TWO

When I got to Houston, I went by Michael because it was my brother's name. He died in Junior High, some odd bone disease that he could never shake. Funny how that works. Two brothers, God decides to kill one. He took the good one. I can't imagine why. I never tried to figure out God. Killed my little brother, who never did anything wrong. He liked playing with G.I. Joes. Wanted to be a soldier so he could "stop the bad people."

All I ever wanted to do was join my dad in the family business. God kills my brother. And yet lets that priest do unspeakable things...So the DDs...about them....Jesse loved all of them. But he spent most of his time with me, Louis, and Mare. Louis was kind of a know it all dick. Always thought he was the best handicapper. Never stayed sober. Not sure how he kept his job; he was drunk all the time and always at the track or the bar. But he would write one article a month for some glitzy magazine, and they seemed to love him. He obviously made good money, even with the child support.

I never really trusted him, but then, who was I to judge? It's not like I had many friends, and he was as close as any. And I will give him a little credit; he talked me into writing. Told me several times I had a great story to share. So I started this journal. It's just another thing that keeps 31 from coming each day. Louis and I got closer after Jesse showed up.

I think Jesse wanted it that way. He had his reasons. Jesse was always right. And we had some good times.

When good Louis was around, he really was a lot of fun.

It irritated me that he was always hitting on Mare, but then almost all of us did. Plus, she was a redhead. And I loved redheads. But I never pushed it. Did not want to screw up the table dynamic. And there were plenty redheads out there for an old man. And you know what Louis told me once? He never did with Mare, either. Gained a little respect for him that day. Because with Mare, any of us could have. I know Fat Johnny had spent a fair amount on her. Mare was in her mid-30s, devastatingly beautiful. The age and hard living had crept into her face, but her milky skin was still nearly flawless, her green eyes always disarming you. She had some light freckles, and her auburn hair hung deep over her shoulders. Her body was still extremely tight, and her doctor-bought breasts screamed from behind whatever she was wearing. She always picked the perfect colors to match her hair, eyes and skin. She knew how to look beautiful. She had to. It was her job.

Mare worked at the Silver Cup, the strip bar across the street from the track. She would hang with us during the day, then work until closing -- and sometimes after. She was worried that at some point she would be relegated to afternoons -- the retirement time for strippers -- but she still had enough to compete with the younger girls. Mare had gotten pregnant at 15, and started stripping and doing what she called "side business" as soon as her daughter was born. Lilly was a beautiful, smart kid. She spent a lot of time with her grandparents, who lived nearby, but Mare made enough money to send her to private school.

Mare's only goal in life was to make sure her daughter would never have to live like her mother. For the longest time, it was looking good. Lilly made terrific grades, was brilliant at science and wanted to be a doctor. Mare did everything to keep her away from the life that was paying for all of it. But after Lilly's 16th birthday party, a drunk, high Mare passed out, and one of her clients who had scheduled an appointment got angry when he couldn't wake her. He found a sleeping Lilly, raped her repeatedly and pistol-whipped her almost to death.

The man was a big time businessman in the Hispanic community. Jose something or other. Big, slick Mexican who showed up at the track sometimes in cheap suits. Married. Four kids. Went to St. Joseph's church, where he was a big noise. The story made all the papers and newscasts. Nobody believed such a righteous man could have done it. He was convicted and sent to Huntsville State prison, but his prison sentence was light. It was a whore's daughter, after all. Most people blamed the mom as much as they did that piece of shit. Big topic on political radio.

His stay in Huntsville was short and painful. They found him in a cell with a cane shoved so far up his ass it pierced his heart. No, it wasn't me. I told you what I was saving Number 31 for. But I still had people on the inside who owed me. I will probably tell you about them later. Not sure. Still trying to decide how much to tell you about the family. But I went to my friends in this case and asked for a favor.

They paid off big time. That made all the papers, too. And yes, Mare suspected I had something to do with it. She never thanked me, but she did hug me once, and tell me she appreciated me. That was enough.

When Lilly recovered, Mare sent the girl to live with her grandparents permanently, but Lilly was never the same. A year later she took her own life. Mare's own life fell apart from there, a daily dose of gambling, drinking, drugs, dancing, and late night appointments. Those bright green eyes almost always looked empty after that. Some days you could see the guilt as plainly as if she were talking about it. Jesse brought life back to those eyes for a while, like he did with a lot of us. We all flirted and hit on her, but oddly enough, Louis and I never pursued it. Any one of us could have had her for a price, but something about that just didn't seem right. So we would play our little games and they never meant anything. Maybe some of the others at the table did. But somehow, it was different for us. Another odd thing Louis and I had in common. I did not have much left in the way of emotions, but I hurt for Mare after she lost Lilly. That girl could have been something. And Mare had tried so hard to keep it all away from her daughter, only to have it explode in the worst possible way.

Pete was a quiet, mousey man who did something in oil and gas, like most people in Houston. He would spend hours on the phone, presumably handling his business. He kept to himself a lot. He never really trusted anyone, and always seemed out of place. But he also acted like a guy who knew it was OK to be out of place at that table. I always suspected he was gay, but he never talked about it and we never asked.

Frankly, we didn't care. A lot of people in Texas did. The state was terrific in so many ways, but backwards in so many others, especially tolerance. Houston was an extremely tolerant place inside the loop, but in the suburbs -- where the track was located -- people weren't always so understanding. Maybe that's why Pete did not tell us.

Big Jim was pure Texas cowboy. A mountain of a man at 6'5" and a rock-hard 240 pounds, he was a visual specimen. A former football player at the University of Houston, he now did collections for the local bookie at the table, a man we simply called Spider. Big Jim had the stereotypical drawl and called everybody "hoss." The voice always seemed out of place, because Big Jim was black. But he was as country as they come, growing up on a catfish farm. Considering his size and what he did for a living now, he was as nice a human being as you would ever meet. Jim had a country code that meant he opened doors for ladies, always called me sir and always smiled. It was hard to imagine him collecting from deadbeats, but they always paid, and Big Jim never had to hurt anybody. To be honest, I don't think he could have. Which made it strange that he was hooked up with Spider, a slick, somewhat greasy bookie who hid his business behind a popular kolache shop. He always wore turtlenecks, a giant Star of David and big, bug eyed sunglasses. I had seen a million like him in New York, even done a job or two for them. But I liked Spider. Like all of us, he had a weird connection to the other DDs and a code. He never accepted bets from the table. He would politely refer anyone who wanted to make a play to one of his competitors. And he looked after Big Jim like a father.

The Pakis were a married couple. They were both from Pakistan, quiet, respectful. They chatted amongst themselves in their native tongue a lot. Their names were too long for us to ever learn so we just called them Pak Man and Pak Woman. Nobody had any idea what they did or where their money came from. But they were first to buy a round for the table, even if everyone was losing. And they always asked about everyone's family. Good people. Pak Man twitched a lot, always looked over his shoulder. I had seen that look 1,000 times. The look of a man on the run. Still, he seemed comfortable here. It seemed more like habit.

Bernie was a dentist who owned race horses. His wife pretty much ran their practice now, so he spent his time with us. He hated being a dentist. He had long, thinning hair and wasn't much to look at. He whined constantly about being a dentist, and what a crap job the trainers were doing with his horses. He had one winner's circle picture he carried with him everywhere. He had owned twenty horses in his life. That was the only time one of them finished first.

Sophie was a sweetheart who had a bad gambling problem. She owed everybody at the table money. She worked as a waitress at one of our hang outs -- The Finish Line Bar. She had once worked in a law firm and been married to a really nice man whose name escapes me. He visited the track a couple times. But the gambling bug got her bad.

She lost several thousand dollars in a poker room, then got caught blowing a guy in the bathroom to get more chips. The nice husband found out, took their kids away and she had not heard from him since. We all knew she wasn't going to last long here, either, but Jesse's winning streak wound up saving her.

Finally, there was Big Paul and Little Paul. The names didn't really fit; the older Paul was in his 50s, thin, gray. He looked like an AIDS patient. Little Paul was in his mid-20s, big, bulky and already getting quite fat. But he had been Little Paul since he was a kid, when he was just Big Paul's scrawny son. Big Paul had his own law firm, and Little Paul had become his partner right out of law school. The business had become so big they had farmed it out to a massive team of lawyers and instead spent every day at the track. The Solander Law Firm handled more divorce cases than any in Houston. The man behind it and his ever-expanding son hardly ever saw a case anymore. They spent their days with faces buried in the Racing Form.

It was this group I saw every day. I always was part of a family in New York, but considering what I did, I was close to only a few of them. This was different. These were my friends. We spent every day together and many times every evening drinking somewhere. It was strange, but this odd collection of misfits appealed to me. I had every intention of becoming No. 31 at some point. But seeing them every day made me keep putting it off. They had become an odd type of family. If one of them missed a day, we would always check in with them and make sure everyone was OK, especially Mare or Sophie. If there was an empty chair at the table, we all felt a little bit empty, too. Many others had come and gone, tried to become part of the DDs. But there was something about our group. You either fit in right away, or you simply wandered off somewhere else. Jesse fit in from the beginning.

BOOK FIVE: THE GOSPEL ACCORDING TO LOUIS CHAPTER THREE

So I mentioned I am a little drunk. Things tend to get out of order. I think I would rather just tell you one of my favorite Jesse stories than keep beating myself up right now. I do want to apologize. I'm a better writer than this. I have won a lot of awards. I just can't tell this story sober. Not after what happened on the boat...But no, not yet. I will tell you more about Jesse later, but he was always trying to get us to do good things. Be good people. I hated that, but he made us so much money....

It was Christmas. Jesse had suggested we go to Shining Star and volunteer to help feed the homeless. By then we did whatever Jesse said. He was making us a small fortune for us, so we all felt like we could not say no. And hell, doing a good deed every now and then was kind of Jesse's MO. It did not mean much to me, of course. We had done some other things -- donate money to an at-risk kid's school, cancer research, AIDs research. This was the first time we volunteered our time. It turned out to be a bad idea.

So our silly little group of degenerates was there, serving soup and turkey to a weird collection of lost souls. The homeless aren't what you think. Many of them are good people who just had things fall apart. Maybe they got into drugs, trouble with the law. Lost their jobs, lost everything. They weren't bad people. Somehow they survived on the streets of Houston, where most people would ignore them.

Some of them were quite funny. One guy always had a "will work for beer sign." And yet others would hit you with the same old story about how they were trying to get to Louisiana with their wife and child and the car broke down six blocks away. Some even carried broken fan belts to make their point. I would always ask to see the kid or offer to fix the car. That always chased them away. My other favorite line was when they would ask for money and say they were broke, I would always respond with "I'm $150,000 in debt. You got me beat brother."

I did not see them much anymore. I only went to the magazine offices, which were downtown, once a month or so. Most of the time I would just send my stories in from home. The track was a good half hour from downtown, and I lived near it, so I did not get to the city very often anymore. When I lived downtown, I got to know some of the homeless who lived on the streets near me. I would help them out. But then the ex kicked me out, and I wondered what happened to those people. They were good folks. It's the crazies you have to worry about. Many have serious mental issues, with no access to proper treatment or medicine. They scream at nothing. They fight ghosts. And sometimes they are just flat out dangerous. And that's where it all went wrong.

They called him Crazy Charlie. He looked like a homeless Magic Johnson with a long, dirty beard. Everything about him was dirty. Matted hair, rotted jacket...what teeth he had left smelled of death and spewed puss. He would be calm, then suddenly start screaming. Sometimes he would do worse. He would get arrested, or sent for a psych evaluation, but he always wound up back on the street. The kind of person nobody wanted. It was easier to just cycle him back out there and let him be a problem for someone else. On this day, he was our problem.

I was never really sure what Michael did for a living until I got his journal. He had hinted more than once that he had been a very dangerous man at one time, and I believed him. He was mid-40s, but in outstanding shape. He was always impeccably dressed, his clothes too loose, just in case he ever needed to get in a scrape. I'm pretty certain he always had a weapon on him. He was tall, strong, with slicked back black hair that was greying on the sides. I always thought if Ray Liotta and Al Pacino had sex, Michael would be their kid. I don't think he respected me, but I do think he liked me. I tried to get him to tell me his story many times. He would just flash that sardonic smile and laugh.

Eventually he did start writing notes; I think he was going to tell the story himself, but then how I got it...well, you will find that out. It was good stuff. Better than my writing. I can still see that smile, like he always had a secret and always knew what we were thinking. It wasn't until I read that journal that I realized it was true. It was that weird, wicked smile that was both comforting and at the same time disturbing. And maybe it was that smile that led Crazy Charlie to suddenly swing at Michael. A man who wielded a blade in ways I could never imagine was chopping up a turkey. Michael was just smiling, enjoying his work. But then Charlie started screaming again. The nice lady in charge of the place politely asked him to calm down or he was going to have to leave. She called for security, and three big, volunteer guards started to quickly approach.

Charlie had other ideas. He stared at Michael with a deep contempt, as if everything wrong in his world was on the dapper looking man chopping up his turkey. It happened fast. Charlie suddenly jumped across the serving table, sending dressing, soup and turkey everywhere. He took a long, surprisingly powerful swing at Michael and screamed at him. "God is a fucking liar! YOU are a fucking liar!"

Michael's first instinct was to sharply bring the blade into Charlie's throat and solve society's dilemma with the homeless man instantly. Instead he simply ducked the punch and raised the knife in a threatening manner. Even though he might have been the worst of us at one point, Michael knew how to defuse a situation without it escalating. Most times, anyway. Not this one. Charlie's eyes got big, and started to step backward, something akin to fear in his eyes.

Pete, however, possessed none of Michael's ability to prevent a mess. He blindsided Charlie with a deep right that instantly shattered the tattered man's jaw. Charlie collapsed in a pile of filth. The security guards, confused, suddenly went after both Pete and Charlie. The homeless do have an odd code. They will fight each other, but they will also pull together to protect each other as well. A homeless man they called Skippy immediately threw his soup in Pete's face. A woman they called Linny The Mexican suddenly jumped on Pete's back. The security guards had no idea what to do now. And then all hell broke loose. Filthy street trash were all going after Pete. Big Jim suddenly started throwing bodies left and right. And there was Jesse, trying to get everyone to stop. And Linny bashed him over the head with a soup bowl.

Michael grabbed her by the hair and had smashed her face into the table before Jesse's body hit the floor. Linny's dirty face exploded in a mass of blood, teeth and filth. And then Michael's art was on full display. He broke an arm. Smashed a nose. Dislocated a shoulder. He resisted the temptation to slit every throat in the room. The knife was in his teeth, his eyes blazing, a menacing devil who lived for this. Yet the homeless saw that every day. For them, it was just another crazy.

Somehow I had gotten into it with a dirty old woman who kept hitting me with her cane. It didn't hurt, but after about five strikes I had enough. She was so light. When I hit her, I could feel her fragile body collapse. They called her Mouse Lady, because she kept a bunch of mice with her at all times. Several went scurrying and flying as she hit the ground in a heap. About then the police arrived, and in the confusion, Michael was gone in a flash. He knew how to disappear quickly. He had apparently gotten Jesse out with him. I was bleeding from being blindsided by a turkey leg. It was the director of Shining Star, blaming me for hitting poor Mouse Lady.

Pete was a bloody mess. Little Paul had gotten the worse of a table over the head. Crazy Charlie was on the ground, not moving. Big Jim didn't have a scratch. I couldn't see Spider or the Pakis. I assumed they got out OK. Sophie and Mare had apparently gotten out with Jesse. In fact, it looked like everyone had gotten out except a few of us.

So Pete, Jim, Little Paul. and I spent a night in jail for trying to do something nice. Big Paul showed up the next day, not a scratch on him, and bailed us all out. Seven homeless were hospitalized. Big Paul offered to pay the hospital bills for all of them. The charges are still pending, even as I write this. Thank God it doesn't matter. Maybe that's a poor choice of words.

Anyway, that's the day when I finally decided to quit trying to do anything for anyone else. Take care of myself. Leave the good deeds to others. The day a director of a homeless shelter hit me over the head with a turkey leg, and yet I wound up in jail. Hell, I was already like that. Just a convenient excuse. Sorry, I'm a little drunk.

BOOK SIX: THE GOSPEL ACCORDING TO LOUIS CHAPTER FOUR

The wins kept coming. Jesse was adamant about us keeping things quiet. He did not want prying eyes knowing we were leaving with a lot of cash. If we hit a ticket that was more than 300-1 and paid in excess of $600 -- or anything over $5,000 -- we had what was called a "signer," where the IRS required us to report the winnings. Jesse suggested we let Pete and Paul Jr. cash the tickets, because they made the most money outside of the track and already itemized their taxes. It was an important part of cashing big tickets, one we were getting delightfully familiar with. I will never forget that day, although it did not start out all that well. Bernie actually had to practice dentistry that morning and was in a bad mood.

"I need to hit a big one, guys. I can't deal with this anymore." He took a deep drink of his vodka Diet Coke. It was his go-to drink. "Kid comes in today...hasn't brushed his teeth in weeks. I'm looking at his mouth and it's full of Fruity Pebbles. Fucking disgusting. This is my fucking life. Picking Fruity Pebbles out of this nasty little kid's fucking molars." Pak man laughed and said in his thick accent, "Thanks Bern. I will never eat Fruity Pebbles again." We all got a good laugh, but Bernie simply wasn't in the mood.

"I need something big," he said. "My horses can't run; my wife wants to hire help since I don't want to be there. Let's do this today." It was

Spider who suggested the day's big play. "Want a big score? Santa Anita has a $400,000 pick six carryover."

The pick six is a bet that requires picking the winner of six consecutive races. If someone doesn't hit the bet, it carries over. It is the best path to a big score. The bet had already carried over for three days. Jesse was a little hung over. He was wearing sunglasses and a University of Houston baseball cap. I was wondering why he was suddenly repping my alma mater, with the interlocked UH logo. It was a nice hat. Wish I had one like it. Mare walked gave him a hug. It was clear they were getting close. "You good?"

"Oh yeah," he said. "Give me the Form and I will take a look." The Racing Form was the racetrack bible. It included detailed "past performances," basically the history of each horse. Each line in the Form provided details of each race, and picking the winners was like solving a puzzle. You analyzed the performance of every horse, tried to get a sense of how they would run that day, and how that might impact the other horses. Then you made your best possible guess as to the outcome. It was meticulous. It was challenging. And all of us loved doing it. Most of all, we loved being right.

Big Jim was already drunk. It was 11:30 in the morning, and he had started drinking straight Jack at 11:00. Usually when Jim was drunk that early, he either had a collection that had not gone well, or he was feeling bad about whatever it was that landed him working for Spider. This day it might have been both. "Jess can I ask you something?" His drawl always got worse when he was drinking. Jesse was clearly hurting and didn't want to talk, but he liked the big cowboy.

"Shoot," he said, never taking his eyes off the past performances for the third race. "What are you do'in in Houston, Hoss? Where were you before?" Jesse smiled. It was impossible to irritate him, even though we tried. Me most of all. "Chicago. Was on my way to New Orleans. Decided to stop here. Then I liked you guys. So thought I would stay. Simple as that." Pak man weighed in. "Like us enough to hit this ticket."

Jim nodded, like that answer made perfect sense. "Well, I appreciate you being here, hoss. Means a lot to me." Jesse took a deep swig of wine, smiled at the big fella and started making notes. In my head, I kept hearing the ZZ Top song I had loved for years. "Jesus just left Chicago...he's on his way to New Orleans..." And then "Waitin' on the bus." I liked that song better. I sang them both when I fronted The Dangles in high school. Good times.

Jesse had answered Jim the same way he answered everything. Jesse asked us about ourselves all the time, and was constantly giving advice. But learning anything about him was a chore. He simply did not like to talk about himself. I got the sense Mare was learning a lot about him, but to the rest of us, he was still a mystery. He was brilliant at picking horses. He was always calm and friendly. But we knew little about his past or why he was really here.

Meanwhile, a race was about to go off in New York. "I like the superfecta here," Spider said. It was three minutes to post. That was something you had to be careful with. Races were coming fast and furious. If you tried to bet every track and every race, you simply could not keep up, and your money disappeared fast. Jesse had taught us patience. Spider had picked out a race most of us would have never looked at. Apparently Jesse had.

Jesse never looked up from the Form. "The 6 horse wins," he said. "Key him on top of the 2-3-7-9." A superfecta required hitting the top four finishers in order. Jesse's bet meant the 6 horse had to finish first. Any three of the other horses in the bet could run second, third and fourth in any order. Based on a $1 wager, it would cost $24.

"Those are all bombs," Spider said. "The 6 is 15-1. I like it." By now, we would just bet what Jesse said. We had a table pool that we all put money into at the beginning of the day. Spider made the table bets. We had quickly learned to make the same bets ourselves on the side. The only one who didn't was Sophie. She would put her $100 in the pot. Even with all we were winning, it was all she could afford. I just assumed what she was winning at the track she was throwing away at the poker room or playing slots in the bar. For some reason, "game rooms" had popped up everywhere in Houston. They had found some loophole where you weren't technically playing for money, but everybody knew you were. Sophie wasn't good at those, either.

The table dynamic had changed significantly. Before, we would all throw in a horse, maybe argue a little, and then I would break the tie. But now we just did what Jesse said. And it worked. Jesse would suggest two or three bets a day. He was never wrong. Never. At first, we kept betting

42

on the side on our own on other horses. As usual, we were hit and miss. Jesse's plays ensured we would make a profit. But after a few weeks, we would just drink, BS, and wait for Jesse's plays.

And we were rolling. In just over three weeks, we had cleared over $20,000 each. On this day, Jesse took us to a new level. It started with the New York superfecta. The 6 horse, Rhinestone Cowgirl, wired the field. The 9 finished second, the 3 third and the 7 fourth. Boom. Our $1 table ticket paid $3,800. That one we split 13 ways. All of us had the ticket on our own as well. Except Sophie.

But this day had a different feel. I had bought an extra one for her and did not tell her. When I gave her the ticket, her face lit up in a way I had never seen. Hell, it was only an extra $24, and it just occurred to me it would be a nice thing to do. Damned Jesse. Probably his influence.

Sophie wasn't beautiful. She was mousy, with short brownish hair framing a cute face. She wore spectacle-like glasses. I always thought she looked like a sexy librarian. She always dressed plain, even when she was working the bar, which probably cost her tips. Today it was a nondescript brown blouse with tan slacks and brown loafers. She was short, with small breasts, but had an underrated body. Truth is, most people would never get that far. Sophie would not stand out in a crowd. She had plain brown eyes that were nothing special. She was a nice, safe, 5 or 6. But as Paul Sr. liked to say, "she was a racetrack 9." I had not noticed the body myself until she gave me a warm, strong hug. For the first time I realized how attractive she could be if she put some effort into it. We gave our tickets to Pete and Paul Jr. to cash, kicked them ten percent as a fee and waited for Jesse's next play.

Sophie, for the first time anyone could remember, bought a round for the table and a round of fireball shots. Her face was glowing. I think it was the first time I ever saw her happy, saw her smile. Maybe that "not beautiful" comment wasn't fair. Maybe I just didn't notice until now. She had a wonderful smile. It was awesome to see it. Sophie usually worked nights at the Finish Line. She did not talk much, and almost seemed out of place in our group. We just always saw her at the bar before she joined the DDs. She would get us a few extra drinks, so we invited her out, and she never left, even though she was always kind of an outsider. For as much as we flirted with Mare, we never bothered Sophie. Yet finally, and really for the first time, she seemed like part of the family. And I wanted to flirt with her. I wanted to get to know more about her.

Jesse had a lot to do with that. There was something about him -- other than the winning tickets. It was something almost regal, even for a guy who looked like a Sons of Anarchy extra. He had a way of making people feel good about themselves. Sometimes it was that smile, like with Jim. Sometimes it was the way he laughed at our jokes. And always it was about him winning us money. He seemed completely comfortable with his place in the world. He was always talking about doing good things, and how much better the world was when you made somebody else happy. He would get in deep conversations with the others at the table about god knows what. I was not that interested at first. It was all about the money at the beginning. No matter how he did it, he made people

44

happy. And boy, was he doing that with us. It had made him our table leader.

I wasn't crazy about that. I had always thought of myself as that guy. But seeing Sophie truly happy for the first time since I had met her made me accept it more than ever. Yeah, I had always had a thing for her. I guess I realized it that day. But I never let a woman come between me and my gambling. So I just didn't pay attention. I just ignored it. Then again, maybe it took both of us winning to change that. Everything would change that day. Our long-term fortunes. My feelings for Sophie. Her feelings for me. And it all started with a few simple words from Jesse.

"I can hit this with a $128 ticket," he said, referring to the Santa Anita pick six. It was matter of fact, confident. None of us questioned it. Pete just took $128 out of the table till, made the bet and brought the ticket to Jesse, who for one of the rare times since he had been there turned stern. "One ticket. Just this one. If we hit it 13 times in the same place, we are going to arouse suspicion. No side bets. If I am right, we are taking the whole pool anyway."

So we did not question it. We did however, take the same horses in our pick six and bet the late pick four. We all hit that, including Sophie, for another $10,000 apiece. But we are getting ahead of ourselves. Regardless, that should give you an idea how big the pick six payoff was that day. It was a life-changing score, the kind every horseplayer hopes to get just once.

Jesse's ticket was pretty simple. He had two horses in each race of the sequence on a $2 ticket for 64 combinations, making the total $128. All we needed was for one of our two horses in each race to win. That simple. Still, the odds were against us. Most major syndicates spent thousands of dollars, using multiple combinations and tickets to make sure they cover as many possibilities as possible. As simple as it sounds to have two horses in each race, the reality is you are more often than not wasting money. It would be like sitting a poker table with $128 when everyone else had $4 or $5 thousand. But if you were good and a little lucky... We knew Jesse was good. The only question was could we be a little lucky.

In the first race, we had the even money favorite and a 20-1 shot named Candace Glenn. The horse had only one start and had not run well. But horses often improve dramatically in their second start, and Candace Glenn did, winning by three. The favorite was nowhere to be found, which was odd. When Jesse used more than one horse, they usually ran 1-2. But for our purposes, we only needed winners. And we were 1-for-1 with a horse that paid $42 to win and likely knocked out a lot of people. The final pool for the pick six was in excess of a million dollars. This was as good a start as you could hope for. And for some reason -- maybe it was Jesse's unwavering confidence -- it seemed like the day was going to be something special.

By now, we were all drinking heavily, except for Sophie and Mare. Sophie had to tend bar at the Finish Line. Mare had to dance at the Silver Cup. The races would not conclude until after 6 p.m., and both had to be at work at 5. If we were alive to the last few races, a lot of texting would

46

be involved. No matter what, it was going to be an interesting day. I had visions of going to the Cup, ordering champagne and taking some hot young thing to the VIP "anything goes" room. For $300, you could get in, and for another $200, you could get anything you wanted. And yes, I had been there many nights after a good score. Just never with Mare. It didn't seem right.

Race 4 (the second of our sequence) was a no-doubter. Our horses ran 1-2 all the way around the track, with Vinny's Vision pulling away to win late at 5-1. Two for two. As a table, before Jesse, we had only hit one pick six in our lives. We spent $30, and heavy favorites won every race. We got back $89 total. We could have done it for $6, but I insisted on throwing in a few more horses. We celebrated, but we spent more on alcohol in an hour than we won on that bet.

Today was going to be different. With a 20-1 and 5-1 already home, we just needed to hit to get a solid score. With one more longshot, it could be a monster. That longshot came in the next race. Banadel was the 1-9 favorite. The horse had won its debut by 15 lengths for a powerful barn, with a Kentucky Derby winning trainer who always had good horses. He looked like a future superstar. He now faced a field full of horses each with one career win, looking for their second. Ron's Revenge was the other horse we used. He was 1 for 26 lifetime and had been facing easier horses. He usually earned a piece of the purse, with a lot of seconds and thirds, but was never really a threat to win. I thought we could have left him out. Banadel looked unbeatable. It was only a six horse field, which made Banadel look even better. Ron's Revenge was the longest shot on the board. I thought it was stupid to use him, but I knew better than to question Jesse.

Because funny things can happen in a horse race. Horses are a lot like humans. Sometimes, they aren't in a great mood. Sometimes everything goes wrong. Sometimes, it's just not their day. It wasn't Banadel's. He reared at the start, immediately starting six lengths behind the field. Meanwhile, three other horses collided out of the gate, leaving Ron's Revenge on an easy early lead. Banadel recovered and began to rush to the lead. But one of the other horses -- agitated from the rough start -- drifted out badly and cut off Banadel, who immediately checked and dropped to last again.

Meanwhile, Ron's Revenge kept chugging along. He opened up a two length lead on the field turning for home. Banadel began to charge up menacingly on the outside, but once again was cut off by another horse. It really was turning into a nightmare for him. At the top of the stretch, he finally got reset, got in the clear and took off like a rocket. He managed to get into a photo finish, and two jumps past the wire he was six lengths ahead. Banadel was the best. But not when it counted -- the one moment they crossed the wire. It just wasn't his day. But it was becoming ours.

The day belonged to 30-1 long shot Ron's Revenge, who won by a nose. He was also the first horse in our pick four sequence, which had started with that race. If we could hit both...well, we knew we were sitting on something potentially incredible. I knew Banadel would go on to be a special horse someday. But on this day, he was second best. "About time Rodriguez did something right," I said, referring to the jockey. "Dude has cost me more money than all my ex-wives combined."

One truth at the track -- we always blamed the jockey no matter what. Or gave him too much praise, depending on the result. It was like a quarterback in football. Edgar Rodriguez was one of those who I was always out of sync with. If I liked his horse, it ran like crap. If I didn't, the horse would beat me. I wasn't a fan of Edgar's. Today he was in my cool book. I didn't like many jockeys. They were risking their lives every time they got on a horse, but they also were dumbshits. There were very few I trusted. Edgar wasn't one of them.

After that, you could feel the buzz. Halfway home to a lifetime score. It would not mean a lot to some of the people at the table who had a lot of money. But to me, Mare, Sophie...it would be life- changing. If we hit it, of course. As if reading my mind, Bernie tapped me on the shoulder. "We got this, man. I got a feeling."

I just smiled and glanced over at Jesse, who was casually leafing through the Form. We all kicked ourselves when we saw the pick 3 payout. Our three winners paid almost $5,000. We consoled ourselves with the fact we had all played the late pick 4, both as a table and individually. And we were off and running with the 30-1 shot. But one miss in the next three races and that would mean nothing. The pick three would have been a nice saver for the day. Bird in the hand, man. And we could have done it for $6. It's always the bets you don't make that you regret. Or the ones you win where you did not bet enough.

The next race was not as dramatic. We had left out the slight favorite, Marhol, who went off at 4-5, and used the second and third choices, Bartholomew at 5-2, and Stan's Wish at 7-2. Stan's Wish took the lead early and never looked back, and we were two races away. For that race, once again it was our best possible result. It had been that way every race. That was a good feeling. Each one knocked out more people with potential winning tickets. Sophie and Mare left for work, both whispering something to Jesse. Mare smiled at me on the way out. "This is my ticket out of the life," she said. "Bring it home." Sophie gave me a hug and didn't say a word. She had been close to big scores before and been disappointed.

That's when Paul Jr. came over, brought me a shot of Jack. "Let's celebrate," he said. "You and me." I was horrified. "Too soon, man," I said. 'We aren't there yet." This was bad mojo. You NEVER celebrated a win before it happened. Always at the end. But I saved it. We took the shots anyway and celebrated it as the superfecta score from earlier. That's how I justified it. And I wanted to get drunk.

Bernie obviously needed the money as much as we did. He was wandering all over the place. Stalking. Walking in circles. "It is a weird feeling, man," said Bernie to no one in particular. "Knowing we might have something special. Knowing we've already gotten through the hard part. But also knowing if we miss the next two it means nothing." All I could think about was Bernie did not need to mention that. We all knew it. Crap like that could jinx it. Fucking dentist.

Pick sixes paid consolations for five out of six winners. So one more win and we would get back a significant score anyway. But Bernie was right. Miss the next two and nothing that happened earlier mattered. Fucker had to remind us. I wished more Fruity Pebbles on his ass. It was one of the oddities of playing a bet like this. Sometimes, you were out early and forgot about it. But the days you were sitting four out of four, knowing you were close and just needed a break…

We had been there many times, and it almost never worked out. The track was littered with bad beat stories, and we were the kings and queens of them. But things had been different lately, and we all could feel it. This was our day. Our time. The racing gods had picked us to smile upon for a change. I was already thinking about what I might do with my share. Maybe get a new car. Maybe a new guitar. It was our day.

The fifth race of the sequence crushed that feeling immediately. Our two horses were the 4-5 favorite Snapshot, and a 10-1 long shot Invincible Steve, who crossed the wire second. He looked like a winner, but after a long, bumpy stretch duel, Bold Desire, the 3-1 second choice, finished first. Bold Desire was not on our ticket. We were crushed. Jesse just looked up and smiled. "Don't worry, guys. He's coming down."

None of us heard him. Mike just laid his head on the table. Jr. threw a full beer into the glass wall behind us. I just stormed outside, screamed at the top of my lungs in anger. Why us? Why the hell was it not our day? I found a private area overlooking the racetrack, lit up a joint and tried to cool down. The alcohol glow was all over me, but now the anger was rising. "Fuck," I whispered. "Fuck, fuck, FUCK." I stared out at the track. It really was a beautiful facility, with signs all over the backstretch, including one for Jack Daniels. We weren't far from the approach at Bush Airport, so every now and then a giant jet would float overhead. One did just about then, drowning out my curse words.

I had a weird attraction to planes. Always wanted to fly one. Always loved the way they seemed to float across the sky. Always hated one when we had to deal with turbulence. For me, turbulence was like traffic. Unavoidable. But I still went nuts. About then, old man Michael walked out. He sat down next to me and shared a drag. It wasn't great weed, but it was OK. "You might want to come back in," he said. "This might work out."

I didn't really know what he was talking about, assuming he meant we would hit 5 of 6 and get a nice score. When I looked at the TV, however, I saw the numbers flashing. In my gut, suddenly the feeling changed. There was hope. But it was the kind of hope that was tempered. It really was an awful feeling. We had gone from the high of knowing we were going to do it, to the ultimate low, and now a faint hope that maybe we might get lucky.

The "Inquiry" and "Objection" signs were posted, and the head-on replay was being shown. Bold Desire had bounced into Invincible Steve at least four times in the stretch, knocking him offstride. The stewards - who made racetrack decisions and rulings - were looking at the replay and talking to the jockeys. If Bold Desire's unruliness had changed the result of the race, he would be disqualified. Our horse would be placed first. It would be a victory after all. But it took a lot to take a horse down, especially at Santa Anita.

It might have been the longest 15 minutes of my life. The table was dead silent. We could hear others around the track in the background, arguing whether or not the horse should be disqualified. "No way," I could hear someone saying. "No way they take him down." He clearly had a ticket on Bold Desire. My stomach was churning, but then the buzz kicked in. Suddenly I was ridiculously calm. No one said anything except Jesse, who occasionally mumbled it was a "no brainer" the horse would be disqualified. After 15 long, grueling minutes, where we sat and stared at numbers flashing on a board, he was right.

When a horse is disqualified, they take all the numbers off the tote board and it goes briefly blank. That's how I knew, even before the announcer said in his thick South African accent, "ladies and gentleman...we have a disqualification." When the board went dark, I could not help myself.

As calm as I had been, it all came out. "Fuck yeah!" I jumped out of my chair, arms in the air. The high-fives began. Everyone was celebrating. Jesse motioned to us to calm down, that others might be watching. But that was the racetrack. Every race someone celebrated. Every race someone cussed in anger. Every race someone screamed at a TV, yelling at horses and jockeys in another state who could not hear them. It is what we did.

I heard the cussing from the "No way they take him down" guy, who stormed out in anger, his last $5 lost. I stopped long enough to text Mare and Sophie. "5 for 5! 10-1 shot! One more!" I got back smiley faces from both. The one from Sophie made me glow a little extra. I was drunk and high, but I was starting to realize I liked her. I wanted this for her as much as me.

Screw that. I wanted this for me. This wasn't just Mare's ticket out. I was finally going to be able to pay off all the bills my ex had stuck me with. Finally have some breathing room. Finally not be a loser. Just one more race. We just needed one more horse to get home. The race prices became official. Our horse paid $22, and we knew that even 5 out of 6 was going to be a record score. But we all felt like it would be more. We had our luck. Now we just needed to be right. The screen showed the potential pick six payoffs. My heart jumped in my chest when I saw the ones to the 2 and 10 horses, the ones we had in our bet. We had the only live tickets in all of America. Every other horse, next to the number it said "5 of 6 pays…"

For our purposes, it did not matter which one came in first. We would get the same payoff either way. Over $900,000. In addition, several 5 out of 6 tickets. And oh yeah, we had that live pick 4. The last race was for maiden claimers, horses that had never won a race, and were available to be purchased. In essence, the lowest possible quality race horse. It was a full field of 12, and I had the same feeling I always did before the last race of a big sequence -- I wished we had all of them on the ticket.

Poor quality horses were inconsistent, so it was hard to feel too good about only having two of them. The 2 horse was the favorite, a tepid 3-1. He had run three times, leading each time and fading badly late. He would clearly be out front, and the question was whether or not any of these other horses were good enough to catch him. His name was Smirks A Lot. For some reason that made me smirk, too.

The interesting part was we were also alive in the pick 4. It was paying $2,200 to the 2 horse. But to the 10, it was paying over $10,000. That's because the 10 was a 50-1 first time starter called Believe in Me. His works were nothing special, his jockey had one win at the meet in 50 tries, and his trainer had yet to win a race. He was basically a throw-in.

I asked Jesse why he used the 10. He just smiled like he always did. There was something about that smile. It was disarming. It was charming. His teeth were a perfect white. I'm not into men, but his face was beautiful, framed by that long, black hair, even more prominent under the red UH hat. He had a way of making you relax and trust. Part of me hated everything about that. Not today. "Crap race," he said. "We have the only horse that's shown anything, and he's not very good. It would not take much for this horse (the 10) to be a factor. It's the devil we don't know." I smiled back at him, echoing what Bernie had said to me earlier. "We got this."

"We do." He then asked everyone to lean in and listen as he whispered. "Don't celebrate, guys. We don't want people to know what we have here. If we hit this and go nuts, people will notice. Let's keep it between us." We all agreed, but knew it would be impossible. The 30

55

minutes between races was interminable. Pak woman had her eyes closed, swaying back and forth, murmuring what sounded like a prayer. Big Jim was chewing his fingernails off. No one wanted to talk. Finally, Spider started telling some story about Jim's football days. None of us really heard. All I could think about was being so close. So many times I had been right there. We had been right there. It had never happened. Yes, we had some really nice scores since Jesse arrived. But nothing like the potential this one had. I resisted the urge to start counting the money in my head. What I would buy. What I would do. I thought of Sophie and texted her to try and distract myself, but she was obviously busy. I walked outside, smoked a little more, and got as serene as possible. By the time I got back inside, the horses were being led to the gate. We were six long furlongs from doing it. The race seemed to go in slow motion. Smirks a Lot shot out of the gate and immediately opened up three lengths. Believe in Me, like a lot of first time starters from bad trainers, broke slowly and dropped well back. I alternated between watching the two horses. My attention drifted to the 4 and 7 horses, who were second and third, and seemed to be moving pretty well. They would be the threats. Every other horse was just bouncing up and down.

Smirks a Lot still had a nice lead, but he was already shortening stride as the field hit the turn. He had very little left, but the horses chasing him weren't exactly full of run. I scanned the back to see where Believe in Me was, and couldn't find him. That's when I saw a horse in mid-pack on the far outside, making a big move. I quickly picked up the number. It was the 10 horse, Believe in Me. When he swept past the 4 and 7 at the top of the stretch and took aim at the staggering 2, all I could think of was the scene with Richard Dreyfuss in Let it Ride.

"I knew it." Smirks a Lot finally threw in the towel with a 16th of a mile to go. By then Believe in Me was even with him, rolling down the outside. He was still wide, running awkwardly, but he was on his way to an easy, five-length victory. Smirks a Lot stopped dead in his tracks and finished seventh, but none of that mattered. The table was eerily quiet. It was almost relief. I walked outside, lit up what was left of my joint. I stared at a perfect blue sky and let it sink in. I texted Sophie and Mare. "We got it."

Then I let out a loud, raucous scream of joy I didn't think I was capable of producing. It was the single greatest moment of my life. I had never felt joy like that before and damned sure never have since, even though we would have many scores like this. That day was different and would always be special. That was the first time in my life I felt like a winner.

With the pick 4 and pick 6 scores, each of us walked out of the track with a little more than $85,000 after taxes. It was the score of a lifetime, a year's salary for me. And it was only the beginning.

Jesse had a smug look of satisfaction as we discussed the practical matter. Pete would cash the tickets and sign for them. We would get a small chunk of cash immediately and split it up, but the bulk of the money would come in the form of a check, dated three business days later, because the track had to collect the funds from the host track. Pete had set up an account for just this situation. We divided up the cash quietly, and Pete wrote each of us a check dated a week from the score.

"How much does Sophie owe you guys?" Jesse asked. We added it up, and it came to about $2,000. Jesse peeled 100s from his stack and paid all of us what she owed. "You don't need to do that," Pak Woman said. "We don't need that money. She is free and clear with us." Jesse just flashed that smile. "Let's settle her up now. You never know when she is going to need it again." Michael gave me a big pat on the back. "Want to hit the Finish Line? Take Sophie her money?" I had planned to hit the Cup, but this sounded like a better deal. "Absolutely," I said. "First five on me."

Jesse was off to see Mare and deliver her share. Everyone else went home to celebrate alone or with their families. That's when I realized Michael -- like me, Sophia, Mare and quite possibly Jesse -- had nobody else. We got a little closer that day. Even within our family, we were becoming a click, a family within the family. The group that did not have anyone else. We gravitated to each other more than the others, and there was a weird comfort in it. The look on Sophie's face when she saw the check was something I will never forget. She immediately began crying and hugged us both. "I love you guys so much." Her voice trailed off. "So much…"

I was aroused instantly. I was pretty sure she noticed. She wiped the tears away, the smile we had not seen until that day now seemingly permanently plastered to her face. "I will pay everybody what I owe when the check clears." I wanted to tell her, but Michael beat me to it.

"Don't worry about it," Michael said. "Jesse took care of you from his end." She started crying again as a drunk biker across the bar started screaming for another drink. She smiled, wiped her face and grabbed a Lone Star from the freezer and walked away. "Don't you guys leave," she said. She walked away, and I gave Michael a big hug. "Damn man," I said. "What a day."

By now I was almost a zombie from all the alcohol. Michael never seemed to get drunk. He had been at it all day, and could stay here until closing and still be lucid and look like a million bucks. I wasn't that lucky. The Italian smiled at me. We always figured he was mafia, and he never really did anything to change our opinions. I think he liked the mystery of it. "I wish you would let me write your story," I said to him, out of nowhere. I had been thinking about it for days. I guess the buzz made me brave. When I had broached it before, he had become angry or sullen. This time, he just smiled. "Kid, you don't want to write my story. The shit I've done..." His voice trailed off, and the usual sullen mood returned.

"You know what?" I asked. "Just write it down for yourself. It's cathartic. It's redemptive." Michael looked deep in his glass, and fired back straight Jack Daniels. "There's no redemption for me." His eyes glassed over as the opening strains of Ruby Tuesday began to play on the juke box. But he was thoughtful. And I suspected he had been giving it some thought. After a long pause, he admitted he had.

"Jesse said the same thing," he said quietly. "I figure I owe him for today. So yeah, maybe I will write it down." I immediately felt guilty for killing the mood. This was our day. We should be having fun. "If you don't want to show it to me, it's fine," I said. "Trust me, it can be a rush to look at it all in one place. I've seen some ugly things myself, you know." Michael laughed, but there wasn't much humor in it. "You just think you have, kid. But maybe one day I will let you read it. Maybe not. But I will give it a try. And we will see what happens from there." I laughed and popped him on the shoulder. He grinned, but seemed lost in the song. "*Catch your dreams before they slip away...dying all the time. Lose your dreams and you will lose your mind.*"

About then, Jesse and Mare walked in, all over each other and already a lot drunk. Apparently Mare decided to take the night off. She had also given her two weeks notice. Jesse had inspired her, and the money was enough to get her out for good. That made all of us happy. She probably did not know this, but we all rooted for Mare. We knew her past, and we also knew how incredible she was. Mare was impossible for any man to dislike. It was clear she and Jesse were getting very close from the casual way her arm looped low around his waist. Jesse ordered drinks, and like Mike, slammed a Jack in an instant.

I don't really remember when Jesse had switched to Jack. He had been a wine drinker when we met him, which always seemed odd to me. But he drank a lot more now, and like all of us, he wanted to get there fast tonight. We were all already there, but we were headed for zombieland. We were headed for blackout drunk. And that was OK. They sat down next to me, Mare giving me a long, deep hug. She still smelled of stripper soap, but I didn't mind.

And then everything in her world suddenly came together. All the things that had happened. And one more piece of news, one more heavy weight she was carrying. And Mare, who never shared anything, the toughest woman alive, started to soften. Mare, the strongest, maybe the coldest person we knew, a woman who we had never seen cry, suddenly broke down. "I need to tell you guys something.... I wanted to tell all three of you at once..." Michael and I were stunned. Mare was the most unemotional person we knew. Nothing bothered her. The idea of her crying was a complete shock. Jesse just stared at his drink knowingly.

Michael was always the one who diffused things. He tried here. "It's all good, tough girl. Tell us what you need to tell us." She sighed, her ample breasts heaving. She really was beautiful. Something about those green eyes and that red hair. And oh yes, those breasts. "The Doctors think I have breast cancer." The words hung there, and suddenly the mood of the day took a bad turn. Now her tone was matter of fact, and the old, tough Mare had returned. But we could not process the words. "It's just the first round of tests. They haven't confirmed it. But they think I might have it. I have been a little short of breath lately, and had some pain. They aren't sure, of course. But that's what they think. All the signs are there."

We sat in silence for a moment, and Jesse stood up. For the first time, his eyes flashed what looked like anger. He nodded at us, and immediately hugged her. He seemed like he had been expecting this. "The Doctors are wrong," he said. He then put his hand on her chest. "Wow, your hand is so warm," she said. "They are wrong," he repeated.

And the silence. A strange silence, like something significant had happened. Like when the lights went dark on the tote board. It was odd, like someone had suddenly cast a spell. Her entire mood changed, and suddenly she looked like bold, tough Mare again, who never let anything get to her. Beautiful Mare.

"I believe you," she said. Jesse drained another drink. "Come on, honey," he said. "Let's go to your place and celebrate." She smiled, gave him a huge, deep kiss, and they quickly exited the bar. Both of us had no real clue what had just happened. Michael and I just looked at each other, perplexed. We went from joy to emptiness to who knows what in the matter of a minute. And yet strangely, it all seemed OK. Like it had not happened at all.

Sophie came over again. "What was all that about?" Michael just smiled at her. "Nothing, honey. Guess you are down to just us." The biker and a young couple who had been at a table had left, and once Jesse and Mare departed, it was the three of us and the Mexican who worked the grill. "You guys want anything to eat?" She asked. "My treat." I realized I had not eaten all day, but I wasn't hungry. We both refused, so she told Marco to go home, put up the closed sign, and locked the door behind him. She lined up three shots of fireball, then knocked them all back herself.

"Sorry, guys. Have to catch up." She smiled at me, and I realized we were both feeling it. What had taken so long? I guess I realized we both knew we were losers, and would be no good for each other. But now that we had things going our way...Now that we had money.... It didn't take long for Sophie to get as wasted as we were. Michael was as lucid as always, but I was slurring, and my big tell -- I was repeating myself. But Sophie did not seem to mind. Once she started glowing, Michael got curious. For some reason, we had never asked before. I think Jesse inspired us to ask questions.

"Honey, what the hell happened to you? Why are you hanging out with us? I mean at the track, not tonight. I know why tonight. We brought you a big ass check. You are better than us, you know." She thought for a minute, then dropped a sad but knowing smile. "You know what? I love you guys. You brought me the score of a lifetime. So I am going to tell you what happened, but you can't tell anybody else at the table, OK?"

Sophie always looked so worried about everything. Money.

Life. She seemed so out of place with us. But tonight the shots had kicked in. And she was as comfortable as I had ever seen her. Having money will do that to you. "I wasn't always a waitress and bartender, you know. I was, like, important." I loved the way she said "like" too much. "My husband, was like, awesome. Met him at UH. He was like the quarterback. He graduated UH law school, we got married, had a couple kids. Life was like, perfect."

I snickered. "Sounds familiar…" She laughed. God I loved her laugh. I could never remember hearing it before. "I was working as a paralegal at a big firm. Good money. He was a lawyer. Better money." She giggled, like that 18 year-old high school sweetheart. "Yeah so, we were, like, making REALLY good money." Damn. Money meant so much to all of

63

us. I guess I wasn't surprised to hear it meant so much to her. Still, I was getting more aroused by the minute. It was odd, but damn there was something about her telling the story…"Then I got into gambling…" Michael put a hand on her shoulder. Now she was getting emotional. The smile was gone. The laughter was gone. It was as if that phase of her life had happened all over again. She was reliving it right in front of us. And we were spectators.

"I couldn't stop, guys. I was playing online poker and losing thousands. Then I would lose at the track. And then I would lose with Spider betting sports -- before I hung out with you guys. He cut me off. You need to know that. He would not let me get in a big hole… I tried so hard to hide it from Mark. I ran up my credit cards, and was hoping he would never know...God, guys, I was so terrible…" Michael was, as usual, right on top of things. "We've all been there, honey…" She was welling up now. "You know, guys, I never cheated on Mark. Never been with anybody else. Haven't been with, like, anybody else since. But I had such a bad run…" She took another shot. We all did. "I was at this poker room, the Palms? You know it?" We both did. It was the biggest underground room in Houston. All the best players were there. "Wednesday night, they had lady's night. Women played the tourney for half price. And I won. I invested $20 and won over $500. I was so excited. I decided to sit at the 2-5 table." Michael laughed. "Big mistake. That's where the sharks swim."

"Yeah…" she said, suddenly very sad. "You know that guy...the one they call Falcon?" We both nodded. He was a notorious gambler, one of the best in Houston. When he wasn't sloppy drunk, he was a killer as a poker player. And even when he was trashed he was pretty good. Still, he could be a complete dick. Played in the WSOP, loved to intimidate people. Not a cool dude. But not someone I wanted to get in a hand with. Sometimes, sure, if he was trashed and belligerent. Apparently that night he wasn't trashed.

"He was so good...we got in two big hands. He cleaned me out. I had great hands; he had better ones. It was a gut punch." She sighed and took another shot. "So I went on credit for one large. And he took every penny of that, too." She poured us fresh drinks. I wasn't sure I should have anymore but didn't say no. At that point I was passing out somewhere. Might as well be here. "I had pocket aces. I fucked up pre-flop and didn't raise enough. He raised it to $25, and I just made it $50. He called, and the flop wasn't much. Two clubs, though." I laughed. "He was playing those little crap suited connectors." She didn't laugh. "He checked, I made it $150 to go. He snap called."

"Yep," Michael said. "Clubs." She sighed. "The ace of clubs hits on the turn. I have top set. The only way I'm beat..." Her voice trailed off. "And you still have draws to a boat," I said. "You can't fold. But you have to know the way that guy plays, he has clubs..."

"No I didn't," she said. So I bet $200, he raises to $500, I shove, hoping he doesn't have clubs. Kind of thought no way he did..." Michael laughed again. "Let me guess...3-4 of clubs." Now Sophie laughed even harder. "Not even close...3-5. "Of course the board didn't pair, and I lost it all."

She looked forlorn. "You guys have to understand...I couldn't tell Mark. I had nothing left to do. My credit cards were maxed. I had cleaned out savings...And now I owe the room $1,000. I was in total fucked mode. What could I do?" Michael nodded. "Yeah, I know. Been there...We all have kid. You know that, right?" She lowered her head. "How could I?" She was staring at the wall, focusing on nothing. "So you know Checkers? The guy that, like, runs the room?" Everybody knew Checkers. He was a slimy, with a giant nose, and always wore a checkered shirt. I was pretty sure Michael had done side business with him, especially the way his face cringed when she mentioned him. We both nodded.

"I asked to go on the finger for another grand. He said no. But he told me I could be forgiven the grand I owed and he would give me another $200 on top to sit back down if I blew him." Michael sighed. "That's Checkers. If I had a dime for every time I heard that story. Male or female, Checkers doesn't care. Just loves getting blown." Sophie looked horrified. I thought maybe Mike should have kept that to himself.

"You guys have to understand...I was desperate. So we went in the bathroom and I started taking care of him..." She looked sick. Then laughed. "It wasn't all that bad, guys...he was so small...It was like blowing a Vienna sausage." It was our turn to laugh. I never realized what a sense of humor she had. "But as he was finishing, Joey Taps walked in and saw us. And you know Joey worked for my husband. He probably called Mark the second he walked out..." She laughed without humor. "You know what sucks? Well, besides me, I mean...I ran that

$200 back up to $600. And I was free and clear. All for three minutes of nothing." Now you could see the sadness in her eyes.

"When I got home, Mark did not say a word. The next day he took the kids out of school, disappeared and I was all alone. But the worst part...we worked at the same firm. I got fired. And I could not get another paralegal job. He poisoned me with them...I understand him wanting to leave me. But not a firm in Houston will hire me. Everybody knows I blew a guy in the bathroom. Why is that such a big fucking deal? Now I have no husband, no kids, no job. This is the best I can do. Bartending. And I suck at it. They would fire me but they are afraid they would lose all your guy's business. You are the only reason I have a job." Michael had that look. Like he knew the answer to everything. That was Mike. "Why didn't you talk to Big Paul? They could have found your husband, got you your kids back, fixed the whole thing..."

Now Sophie was laughing, this time truly amused. "I know exactly where they are. He took them to Aspen, Colorado. His dad has a monster firm there. Mark always wanted to work for him...It gave him what he wanted all along. We only stayed in Houston because he went to law school here and my family was here." I was pretty much too wasted to talk. Michael was getting close, but asked anyway. "Then why not see them? And he really cut you off over a blow job? Jesus what a dick." Sophie looked him right in the eye, with a self- awareness I had not seen from her before. "Because, Mike...I am a shit mom. I have a ridiculous gambling problem. You both know I will lose all this in a few months...Like, every fucking penny. I was out playing poker until 2 a.m.

when I should have been home with my kids, whether I was blowing Checkers or not. That is what I am. I should not have those kids."

He started to talk, but she interrupted him. "They deserve better. All of them…Come on, my friend. You have to see that." Michael smiled, got up, and gave her a monster hug. He did see it. "Honey, you are better than you realize. I gotta get home." He then gave me a knowing look. "You kids have fun." He left, and Sophie locked the door behind him. She looked at me, and I was more aroused than ever, even though I doubted I would be able to actually perform.

By now it had been a solid 14 hours of drinking and getting high. It would have been poke and hope. But I would be in. "You want to go back in the office?" She asked. "There's a couch…"

"Oh yeah…" was all I could manage. We made love until we both passed out. It was the best day of my life.

BOOK SEVEN: THE GOSPEL ACCORDING TO MICHAEL CHAPTER THREE

So I am not crazy about writing down any of this stuff. So if it falls into the wrong hands, just know it is fiction. About three weeks after that first big score -- there had been at least five since -- I got a text from an old friend and business colleague, Frankie V. You know I don't have many friends. Frankie was my oldest. And he was the closest thing I had to a brother once I lost mine. Frankie was as good as they come. Loyal. Smart. A great businessman. He could also be vicious when it came to protecting his friends and family. So remember that grease ball who raped Mare's kid? Yeah, it was Frankie who helped out with that.

Frankie was No. 2 in the entire business operation. His dad ran things out of New York. Frankie had places in New York, Houston, Galveston and New Orleans. He spent a lot of time in Houston. Had even made it to the track a couple times. Frankie had a lot of businesses -- strip clubs, poker rooms, shipping companies, vending machines. It was the latter that we did business together on. I didn't really do anything, just collected a check every couple weeks for having my name on it. It was a reward for years of service. And loyalty.

Whenever Frankie needed something dicey handled, it was always me he called. Or if it was personal, it was always me. He had promised me three years ago he wouldn't need me anymore, so this one had to be important. The trust between us went way back. I knew no matter what I needed, Frankie would always be there. And vice versa. So when I got the text from an unknown number that simply said "31/44," I knew exactly who it was and what I needed to do.

Frankie had a massive mansion in the glitzy River Oaks area of Houston. It was walled off, with ivy growing on the outside. There was always a security guard at the gate. The guard took one look at me, opened the gate and motioned me forward. I parked in the oval driveway, which circled a massive statue of a dragon. Frankie had always had a weird attraction to dragons. Even played Dungeons and Dragons in high school. No one made fun of him for it.

It was about 10 a.m. Usually Frankie was up by then. But when his "butler," Steven, met me at the door, I knew I had arrived too early. "Mr. V. is still in bed," he said. "But you can wake him." Steven was a ridiculously tall, slow-talking man who reminded me of Lurch. He was dumb, but could be very dangerous. "He meant to call you days ago. He needs your help." Everything was straightforward with Steven.

He put a drink in my hand and led me to the bedroom door. I knocked, then opened it. There was Frankie, rubbing the sleep out of his eyes, lying between a perfect blonde and a dazzling brunette, both naked and passed out. Both girls were clearly in their early 20s, but did not look like strippers. They looked like college girls. Frankie had gotten fat. He already had one heart attack, but clearly had not stopped smoking or drinking. I honestly did not think his life expectancy was much longer, even though we were the same age.

"Scraps!" The girls did not stir as he climbed out of bed, threw a robe over his ample gut and hugged me deeply. "Thanks for coming, Scraps. Been too long." It had been just more than a year since I had visited him at Methodist Hospital after the heart attack. He had promised me he was going to take care of himself. That was one time where he lied to me. He wasn't even close to taking care of himself. He grabbed a bottle of Maker's, poured a glass over ice and downed the whole thing. The room was a mess, with evidence of weed, coke, and of course, lots of alcohol.

"Let's go downstairs, Scraps," he said, his voice raspy from the cigarettes and the tube they had put down his throat during his surgery. Besides getting fat, he had let his gray hair grow out long, and his beard as well. He looked like a mobster Jerry Garcia. But those piercing, intelligent hazel eyes were still there.

"You were supposed to take care of yourself, V.," I said. He just laughed. "That's what I have you for." Frankie lit a cigarette in one hand and a joint in the other, offering me the latter. I gleefully accepted as we started slamming drinks. "What do you think of the blonde?" he asked. "Cute kid," I said. Frankie had been through thousands of them. "At least from what I could see. We didn't get to talk." Frankie bellowed out his big laugh. "I like this one, Scraps." He puffed deeply on the cigarette. "She goes to Rice. I'm paying her way. Wants to be a lawyer."

"What about the other one?" I asked. He laughed again, and it echoed everywhere. "Hell, I don't know. Kerry brought her over last night. She brings a new one to me a couple times a week and we all just have a blast." I took a deep drag on the joint. "Well, if she has any redhead friends…" Frankie laughed deeply and clapped me on the shoulder. "You and those goddamned redheads, Scraps…"

After a long pause, another drink and a few deep hits, he turned serious. "I think I'm going to marry this one." I was shocked. Frankie's first wife had died in childbirth, when his only son was born. He never remarried, and enjoyed the bachelor life. And yet here he was suddenly talking about marrying someone half his age.

"Frankie…" He immediately dismissed me. "That's not why you are here, Scraps. I need you. I know I promised to let you stay out of the game, but I need your help." I wasn't going away that easily. "Let's talk about that girl…" I said. "What are you doing? She's a kid. It's cool to fuck who you want, but marrying her? How well do you know her?"

He smiled, and I could see how much he missed talking with me. "I'm old, Scraps. I'm a mess. I don't know how much longer I have…" He took another deep drink. "I wouldn't mind having another kid. Kerry…she's brilliant. She's fun. She fucks like a porn star. She has a great sense of humor. She gets what I am. I feel good around her." I snorted. "So it's love, is it?" He laughed again. I got the sense he had not been doing that much lately. "Of course not. At my age it's about companionship, anyway. You don't want that sometimes?"

It was my turn to be somber. I never even considered. How could I? How would that conversation go? "So what did you do for a living?" "Um…I killed people. And a cat." Frankie had to know that. "Sure," I said. "But you know what my life has been. I'm OK with the whores.

Take care of business and get out. Just pure transactions. I have my friends at the track for companionship." Frankie laughed. "Like that redhead at the track you hang with? You have to be on that one, right?"

I felt awkward. "Believe it or not, no. She's a friend. Yes, she's a redhead, but there's plenty out there." Frankie got up and pulled a golf club out of a bag that cost more than a lot of cars, and air practiced his shaky, awkward, Charles Barkley-like swing. I had always been the better golfer, and the better athlete. "About those friends of yours at the track..." I interrupted him. "You are keeping the girl out of the business, right?" He was getting impatient. Frankie liked to be the one directing conversation. He was not accustomed to being questioned. "Of course, Scraps. I'm not stupid." I took another deep drink. "I know that. It's my job to have your back." He laughed. "It always has been." Suddenly he was smiling again, looking wistful.

"You always have, Scraps. I will never forget that. And I'm not talking about business...I ran for 1,000 yards thanks to you...old No. 31 opening holes for No. 44...." You were one hell of a fullback. I always thought you would have been even better than me at tailback." I was starting to feel the weed, and the alcohol. "You're right. But I would not have had me to block for me..." We laughed, and Frankie kept working on his golf swing. "Remember those Puerto Ricans?" he asked. I did, because every time I saw him he brought up the story. "Those four guys were going to kick my ass. You told them my dad would do worse to me than they ever could if I got in a fight. "Then you took out three of them in a matter of seconds. Fucking Bruce Lee shit..."

73

He grabbed another drink. They were going down fast. He was starting to slur. "Then you told the fourth one to go get at least ten more friends. Then you pulled that knife out, slashed off half his hair and he took off crying…" I nodded, smiling. "I saved their lives. If your dad had found out…" Frankie put the golf club away. "Those guys lived the rest of their lives never knowing how close they came to disappearing forever," he said. "You had their backs, too. As well as mine."

The way-back machine was in full gear at this point. I had spent enough time reliving the same old shit. "What's this really about Frankie?" Steven walked in with a fresh bottle. Frankie did a line of coke. "Well I need your help, you knew that. But I'm worried about you, too." I was surprised. I had been out of the game for a long time. Everything I did was anonymous. There was no reason for me to worry. Obviously in this business, there's always a chance, but I thought I was well past that. "You and your racetrack buddies are taking a lot of money out of that place…" I smiled. "We've been on a good run." He didn't smile. "You aren't fixing, are you?" The thought had not occurred to me. "No…" I said, suddenly not so sure. "Because we can't bring that kind of heat down on us. You know that." I did know that. And it had not even occurred to me until Frankie mentioned it. "How did you know this?" I asked. He laughed again. "You know I have look outs. Look, I don't know what you got going -- I can't imagine you need the money. If you did you would come to me."

"It's not about the money," I said. "I have more than enough. We are just doing well…" Frankie was getting very serious. This wasn't an old friend. This was a feared colleague making sure nothing could come back on him. It was a role he had to play, no matter how much he might have loved me like a brother. "Well, people are noticing," he said. "I've heard that some of the deadbeats around there are going to rob your group. I would consider it a favor if you and your guys pulled up shop and went someplace safer. Like that bar you all hang out at. Where I can keep a better look out."

I honestly had not realized it had gotten that bad. "I can handle myself." He glared. "I know you can. Pretty sure that Jim character can, too. But what about those ladies? That little brown Indian couple of yours? You think they can stay safe?" I hated it when Frankie was making sense. I wanted to tell him they were Pakistani, but did not see the point. "And that biker character...you've been spending a lot of time with him....is he the one with all the picks?" I was getting uncomfortable, which never happened with Frankie. This felt more like a sit down than a conversation. "He's a betting genius, V. Not sure I know how to explain it, but it's almost mystical...almost like he's some kind of..." Now Frankie laughed out loud. "God? Jesus. The fuck out of here Scraps...He's a fucking con man. Was a poker player and hung out at the tracks in Chicago and got run out of there. He's just a fucking con man. The track is full of them. You should know that."

"He isn't conning me," I said, somewhat defensive. "If it's a con, I'm benefitting." Frankie turned serious again. "Look, Scraps, what the hell happened to you? You spend all your time with these people. You live in a one-bedroom apartment. You are either at the track, that bar, my strip club. Where the hell is all your money?" I was truly drunk at this point. And Frankie was making a lot of sense. He was protecting me. And himself. Just like old times. It felt good. "You have been having me followed," I said. "Not followed," he replied. "I'm just trying to watch your back." I took a deep sip of the Maker's, then refilled the glass. "This is all I have, Frankie. Those goofy friends at the track. I don't need anything more than a one bedroom. I just sleep there. I don't even have a fucking dog." I was uncomfortable. I had seen that look of distrust on Frankie's face. That never ended well. "This is all I need, man. It's all I deserve. As far as the money…" I figured Frankie already knew this, too. "If anything ever happens to me...the West Wall in the bedroom. Give it all a good home."

"Well I am glad you aren't putting it all in the bank," he said. "Just enough to cover expenses," I said. "Not arouse suspicion. How long have you known me?" He starting swinging the golf club again. "I know you aren't cashing any of the tickets, right?" We were starting to sound like an old married couple. "Of course not. Jesus Frankie.

OK, I should not have pressed you on the girl…" He laughed. "Even now, we have to watch each other's backs. You know I'm pretty close to being out of this life, too? This restaurant chain we opened is taking off. Selling all the poker rooms and game rooms to Trevor the Brit. I am going to be totally out of anything illegal in four years. And you already are. So we just have to make it to the finish line." He snickered at his own joke.

He sighed, his giant gut heaving. "So... you guys move to the bar. Watch the races on TV. I got a kid who will run the bets. Vinny Jack's kid? Remember him?" I nodded. "He will cash everything, even the IRS tickets, for ten percent. You can trust him." As much as it would be a hard sell to the others, Frankie was right. It would be safer. Smarter. "That way I can keep an eye on you...watch your back. Look out for each of you. Keep you safe. Like we always do for each other." I just sat in silence.

He had another drink. "What do you say, Scraps? I would feel a lot better about things..." Deep down I knew he was right. "I will talk to everybody." I was uncomfortable, because Frankie was seeing things I wasn't. And he was right. Had I really been out so long I was missing such obvious shit? "Now that's not why you brought me here, is it?" About then Kerry came in, wearing a red nightie. She gave Frankie a big kiss, and held him tightly. "I need to get back to campus, old man," her voice was playful, bright. "And I need to get Kim home. She's all freaked out about what she is going to tell her husband..." Frankie lit up and pointed to me. "This is my oldest friend…" She smiled at me, and I saw immediately why Frankie was stricken. She looked like a young, blonde Phoebe Cates. And she went to Rice? She was way too hot to go to Rice. That was a school for smart kids. No way a girl that hot would be smart enough for Rice.

"Uncle Scraps," she said. "About time I got to meet the best man…" She gave me a hug. Her body was rock hard, and she smelled like roses. I instantly regretted giving Frankie the third degree over her. "Best man,

77

huh?" I asked, smiling at Frankie. He started laughing. "Get outta here, Kerry. Scraps and I have business." She looked at the drink in his hand, and in a flirty way, flicked her hair, turned away and said "I can see that." She looked me in the eyes. "See you soon, Uncle Scraps. I will have a redheaded bridesmaid or two for you…" She floated away, and Frankie looked a little guilty. "Is that all she knows?" I asked. He laughed softly. "So I told her a little about you...nothing business related." We toasted. "I'm happy for you, brother," I said.

It was always odd with Frankie. I could not see him for years, and then suddenly it was like we had never been separated. After Michael died, he was the closest thing I had to a brother. We would fuck with each other, probe each other, but in the end, we would protect each other. And if necessary, avenge each other. It was a strange code we had, but neither would ever refuse the other's request. And I knew it was time to find out was his was going to be. "Now enough bullshit," I said. "What do you need from me?"

For all our dancing back and forth, Frankie had me there for one reason, and it had taken a while to get there. I responded to a text from Louis, asking where I was and if I was OK. By now, it was 3 p.m., we were both drunk, and I had forgotten the table would be wondering where I was. I fired back a simple "All good...got business for a couple days. Be in touch soon." He responded. "Cool. Big day so far. I got your share and bet everything separately for you." I did not trust Louis very much, but I was really starting to like him. We were getting pretty close. It sure was an odd friendship. "Thanks. First few on me when I see you again."

Frankie started talking about his son, Frankie Jr. The kid was in the creative writing program at the University of Houston, and had written several books of poetry and fiction that had been well received. Frankie had tried very hard to keep his son out of the family business. I should mention I was his godfather. Loved the kid but had not seen him in a few years. "He told me he was taking a hiatus from school..." Frankie said. "What the hell? This kid's got talent, Scraps. This life isn't for him. I'm guessing it's just a brooding artist thing, but..."

Jr. had gone to Crystal Beach, where the family owned a beach cabin. Although the term "cabin" wasn't exactly accurate. It was a mansion on stilts. Jr. was holed up there with some friend of his, a petty thief who was trying to become a big noise. And he was dragging Frankie's son into it. And the kid was tagging along, because deep down he wanted to let his father know he could handle things. It was the typical father/son bullshit. But the kid was my godson. Frankie thought he might listen to me. "What's the other kid's name?" I asked.

"Ernesto Rodriguez. Frankie Jr. was banging his sister and these two got mixed up. Ernesto hit one of my shipments. Owes me a nice lick." I sighed, sick to my stomach. "Frankie...I can't light anymore candles. You got people for that. People who can clean this up." There was a long silence. The only sound was the clinking of ice cubes in a pair of drinks. Frankie stared for a while. "This isn't that, Scraps. I wouldn't ask you to do that again. No candle. Hell, my son loves this asshole's sister." We sat in silence for a while. "I need you to show the kid this life isn't for him. Scare the fuck out of the Rodriguez kid but don't blow it for Jr. and the girl. And get my fucking money back."

"Fuck, Frankie," I said. "You ain't asking for much." I looked at the golf clubs, however, and the beginning of an idea crept into my mind. One thing Frankie lacked was subtlety. He could sniff through bullshit in a heartbeat, but he lacked the cunning it took to create complex plans. He was a what you see is what you get guy. He left the cunning to me. "So I have to come up with a way to get your money back, scare the Rodriguez kid, and maybe convince my godson this isn't for him," I said. "That's what you want, right?"

Frankie held up his drink in toast of me. "If you can do that..." he reached under his desk and pulled out a duffle bag. "There's a million in here..." He tossed it to me. I angrily I tossed it back. "This is family, Frankie. I will figure it out. And I don't need the money." He smiled. "Jesus, how much is that con man making you?" I was starting to get that old feeling again. "A lot. I do need one thing, though..." He laughed again. "Anything..."

"I need to borrow your golf clubs for a couple days." He looked surprised. "You don't have yours?" he asked. This time I laughed. "You forget. I quit playing years ago. Only time I play now is when we get together, and then I rent clubs. What's it been? Four, five years?" He looked bemused. "OK. But not a scratch on them...and damned sure no blood..." I took one last deep sip of Maker's. "Not a problem. You might be short a few golf balls, though." He smiled again, positively glowing.

"I'm OK with that." We clinked glasses. the plan already formulated in my head. "I figured you would be."

BOOK EIGHT: THE GOSPEL ACCORDING TO LOUIS CHAPTER FIVE

I did have a job. After I left the newspaper business, I wound up writing for a magazine. One story a month. It was perfect for me. I had a skill. After two minutes of an interview, I could see the story. The poignant parts. The things people would like. So my job was easy. One day with three or four interviews, a day of research, three hours to write. By the time I sat at the computer, I could see the story in my mind. It would flow from there. Editors loved it. Readers loved it. For me, it was like playing poker; learn your opponents and take advantage of them. That's all writing was for me. Learn your subject, make them interesting.

I was a really good poker player, long before Jesse. I would go to the Palms, win a bunch of money, then lose it all the next day at the track. Poker was easy. It was never about the cards. I could sit at a table and in five minutes know everything about everyone there. Who could play. Who would bluff. Most importantly, who to avoid. I had sat at that same table where Sophie lost her money many times. I rarely got in hands with the Falcon. Or another great player who was always there, Golden Guy.

Before Jesse, Golden Guy was the most beautiful man I had ever seen. He looked like a young, blonde, Rob Lowe. Every night he would sit down with two grand. Every night he would walk out with eight or nine. Man, there was something about being at a poker table. The rhythm of chips being shifted. The felt. The social aspect that was only there so some of us could figure out your weakness and take every chip. The rush when you hit your hand. The excitement when the cards hit the table. The deflation when you missed a flop. The good players respected each other. Like I saw in a movie once, sharks don't eat other sharks. Besides, there was no shortage of oil money, drunk doctors and lawyers at that table. And we all took turns feasting.

As good as Golden was, he had the disease. He would be at the track the next day, paying off Spider for his sports bets, which he never won. If he had just stuck to poker, he could have retired. But he had the disease, or more accurately, the disease had him. He once pulled me aside and explained it to me. I had it to, he told me. Winning would never be good enough. We needed action, even on the things we weren't good at. We had the sickness. It was why we couldn't stop later, even when I begged Jesse. We all had it bad. Sophie had it, too, without the skill at something to keep her afloat. And it had ruined her life. If not for Jesse, I think Sophie would have wound up dead.

Since the first big score at the track, I had spent many nights on that couch with Sophie, or at her apartment, or at mine. There was always a weird feeling when you woke up, so drunk from the night before you had no idea where you were. Sometimes it hit you right away. Others it took a couple minutes. Sometimes you woke up embarrassed, but not those mornings with Sophie. Hell, sometimes I was even sober enough to actually finish with her. She didn't mind when I didn't; she clearly got hers. It never occurred to me we should have been using protection. I wasn't always the smartest guy when I was drunk.

So it was around 10:30 a.m, when I got to the track, still wearing last night's clothes. Jesse was the only one there, also still wearing last night's clothes. We gave each other knowing looks, a little fist bump. We actually both had coffee for a change. Every now and then you had to take a day off from drinking. I asked Jesse where the rest of the gang was, and he mentioned something about Big Paul's daughter (and little Paul's sister, of course) getting married. My mind snapped to a vague recollection. I remember being invited, but had forgotten to RSVP. Jesse just politely said "I don't do weddings." I wondered why Sophie had not told me, but I was OK with it.

I wasn't feeling left out at all. In fact, Jesse did not like much on this day in terms of races, so we just talked about some of the others at the table, and how things were going with Mare and Sophie, respectively. I told him I had not been to the Silver Cup since Sophie and I hooked up. He smiled and said I would have to come for Mare's last night. They were desperate for dancers, so she had stayed on a few extra weeks, but worked less and less, danced less and less and really only helped out when things were slammed. She was ready to be out of the place once and for all, but it had kept her afloat when things were bad, so she did not want to leave them in a lurch. Sophie and I had a strange conversation about Jesse one night, and how he could know every race. Always pick the right horse. The right race. It was statistically impossible. We went through every scenario. He was fixing. He was a con man. He was just damned good. Or he was something more.

Sophie was good with that route. "He's my savior, Lou. Look what he's done for me. For all of us. I believe." I laughed. "Well, I don't. But I like money." I shared that conversation with Jesse this day. "Dude, these people are starting to think you are something...I don't know...sacred?" He just smiled, as he always did when I questioned him. "Does it matter what they believe? Belief is our own choice. Let them believe in whatever they want. Just like you believe whatever you want. It's all kind of silly. It's really simple at the end. Do you love your life? Do you have fun? Does it matter how we get there? What we believe in?"

He was right, as usual. For some reason we were both in a small talk mood. "So, Jess...what the hell do you do when you aren't at the track? I mean, for fun. Besides Mare, of course." He smiled again and laughed. "I read. And I watch movies. And occasionally play X box. Same as you." I had never really thought about what Jesse did when he wasn't here. For some reason, everything he said made me feel more comfortable. I was seeing a cool side of him. Maybe these were the conversations the others were having with him. I realized I had been missing out.

"What is your favorite movie?" I asked. "*Last Temptation of Christ*?" He laughed. I think he appreciated my asshole sense of humor. "I hate religious shit. Always so far off of what really happened. And what people should believe.... No, my favorite movie -- and I watch it every time it comes on -- is *Excalibur*. Seen it?" Now it was my turn to laugh. "I love that movie! Did you know Liam Neeson played the knight who accused the queen?" He nodded. Of course he knew that. I started quoting the "charm of making" from the movie..."an-all nathrak, uuus vas bethud…" He cut me off. "Now you are nerding out, Lou." I laughed. He was right. "So why do you like it so much?" I asked.

"Well, I love the "someone will rise and the world will be a good place again" legends. Arthur knows he is just supposed to be an inspiration. But you know what? If he hadn't been such a shitty king, that golden age would have happened right then and there." I had never thought of it that way. And now I was starting to wonder what he meant. "Louis, you know the most wasted emotion we have?" I had no clue, and shook my head. "Jealousy. People are going to do what they are going to do. You being pissed off about it doesn't change anything. Think about it; more than once Merlin tells Arthur that Guinevere is going to sleep with Lancelot. In fact, when they heal Lancelot after the duel, Arthur says 'whatever the cost,' knowing full well that means Lancelot is going to hit it with his wife.

"He knew she was going to do it. If he just accepts that those two needed to get it out of their system, he never thrusts Excalibur into the spine of the dragon, essentially killing Merlin. He doesn't chase off his best knight, or a pretty cool wife who was just intrigued by the same man Arthur loved. In some ways, I think Arthur was more jealous that Lancelot wanted his wife and not him, but that's for another time." He was rolling now. "Look at the consequences. We learn Arthur and the land are one. So for 17 years or so, the land is ruined, thousands of peasants die, all his best knights are killed in a quest that is essentially happening in his head, and all the houses are flocking to the younger, hotter Mordred. All because of jealousy. He got pissed off and petulant because his wife did something he knew she was going to do. And look at the damage it did. He was a fucked up king. Great, you drink from the grail and make everything right after the bulk of your ruling years have been wasted, then you ride out and everybody dies. But someday, a king will come, and the sword will rise again.

"Fuck that. I hope not. That king would suck, too. That sword needs to stay buried. And Arthur should be studied for bad ruling technique. All because he had his feelings hurt. Over fucking jealousy, man. It's poison. They would have gotten it out of their systems after a couple weeks, everybody hugs it out and you move on. You've got bigger fish to fry. Instead, you let all those people suffer. Pisses me off." I was stunned, but interested. "So you would be OK with your wife banging your best knight?" His eyes were alive now. "If the trade-off was all those years of suffering? Hell yes. I would even let them use the royal bedroom. Shake both their hands and bang a chambermaid while I watched them. It's not that important in the grand scheme of things. It's just sex, man. It doesn't mean shit."

"They glorify the ending and all that redemption, but they never needed to even be there, man. Would it have been a better story if he let it go and they rule peacefully for 30 years? And Merlin kills Morgana, and Mordred never happens? Of course not. It doesn't fit the whole original sin thing, man. Fuck it. Jealousy is for the weak. Arthur was weak."

"Damn…" I said, suddenly depressed. And wondering how much of that was intended for me. "Just don't ruin The Lord of the Rings for me…" He laughed. "Don't get me started on how the elves are the bad guys…" Then he dug into the Form. It was time to get to work. The rest of the gang started trickling in, still dressed in wedding clothes. My goodness, Sophie looked terrific. So did Mare. Big Jim had some weird Bolo tie, but he looked like a million bucks. They all did. When Pete came in and showed us pictures of his new Porsche, Jesse gently reminded all of us to keep a low profile. A Porsche was not a low profile.

I noticed something odd that day -- James, a trucker who frequented the track, was staring at us from about 20 feet away. He had a couple musclebound monsters with him, and was especially interested in the Pakis. I didn't think much of it, because a lot of people stared. I should have known something was up then. But I was too caught up in the winning. I wasn't good at noticing things. Think I have mentioned that before. We had another big day, making about $30,000 each, even though Jesse only had a few plays. The side money was good, and I made Michael's bets and exchanged texts with him. I knew he wouldn't be at the wedding, so I was a little concerned. But he said he had a couple days' worth of business. I figured it was best not to pry.

That night I walked over to The Finish Line, suddenly hating King Arthur. I pulled up to the bar, ordered a light beer (it was a non- drinking day) and watched Sophie do her job. I opened up A Feast for Crows and started reading. I was finally going to catch up on the Song of Ice and Fire books. I wondered how Jesse would ruin them for me. I loved

Tyrion. He was my favorite character. Him and Varys, who would have been an outstanding poker player. I loved fantasy. And these books were the best I had ever read.

"You're Louis, right?" A voice came from behind me. It was vaguely familiar. I put down my book and turned around. It was James, who had been eyeing us earlier that day. I nodded, somewhat nervous. I wished Michael was here. I offered to buy James a beer as my heart was suddenly in my throat. I was alone here, and I was not one to put up any kind of fight if things got dicey. I was a coward. He politely accepted and sat down next to me. I motioned to Sophie, who brought him a beer. She smiled at me, which helped me relax a little, but I was extremely tense. Mostly because I was sober. "You guys have been on a good run," he said, as the words trailed off. I did my best to deflect it. "Not bad, but not great. You know, hit and miss."

He laughed. He was a big man, who had once been heavily muscled, but now he had a giant gut to go along with his arms, which were fatty. He was just under six feet, and looked like a sloppy Wilford Brimley, complete with the mustache. I admittedly had not paid him much notice before, but there was something downright frightening about him. Maybe I was thinking of Brimley's role in The Firm. I wondered how Jesse would ruin that movie for me. He sighed deeply, then began talking about his life as a truck driver. He told me his name was James. I think I knew that. He went on and on about how he was always on the road, rarely saw his family, only had a few friends. How he would love to get out of that. After a good ten minute ramble, he got to the point.

"I want in with you guys. Just me and a couple friends," he said. "I don't need much. Just one big score and I am done. And you are doing a lot better than hit and miss. I know the tellers you guys cash with. You guys are killing it. And all we are asking is to be let in on a couple. That's it." I motioned for Sophie to come over, and ordered a Jack and coke. So much for sober day. "That's not my decision to make," I said, telling the truth for once. "Jesse makes the plays. He is who you should talk to."

He took a deep swig. "Oh, I will. But I haven't been able to corner him. Guy disappears when he leaves the track, and you degenerates always have him surrounded when you are there. Maybe you could shoot him a text. Tell him to join us. I don't think I am being unreasonable." I realized then I don't ever remember getting Jesse's number. Hell, I don't know if he even had a phone. I flipped through my contacts. "I don't have it." I motioned to Sophie to come over. "Hey, honey, do you have Jesse's number?"

She picked up on my nervousness. "No, I don't," she said. "Everything OK?" She looked suspiciously at James. I was feeling like the dog that had strayed from the pack and had run into a group of coyotes. One big, Wilford Brimley looking coyote. I nodded to her without saying anything. She brought me another drink, then wandered over to the other side of the bar and whispered something to Dave, the other bartender. Dave was a tall, thin, tatted-up ex con who was also the nicest guy on the planet, other than Big Jim. He looked like Willie Nelson's gay son. He was also the man who sold me my weed. He

90

suddenly took interest in the conversation and James picked up on that quickly.

James smiled, but it wasn't warm at all. It was ugly. "I suggest you find it and reach out. I will be back. My friends are more desperate than me. If you were smart, you would have him talk with us. Soon. Desperate people should not be ignored." With that, he finished his beer, and waddled off. The threat was more than implied, especially when he cast an odd glance at Sophie on the way out. Dave walked over. "You good?" I nodded. "Yeah. But keep an eye on that guy if he comes back. Not sure I trust him." I spent the night with Sophie on the couch, making sure the doors were locked. When we woke up the next morning, my first thought was we needed to find Jesse. Sophie and I went to Mare's, where they were both passed out. A hung over, angry Mare answered the door. "What the fuck guys? Do you know what time it is? What the hell are you doing here?" Mare always responded better to Sophie, so she did the talking. "We need to see Jesse. It's important."

"What makes you think he is here?" Sophie laughed. "Come on, Mare, like I said, it's important." Jesse stumbled in, wearing only Mare's underwear. Man, he was in shape. His body was damned near flawless. Sophie noticed, too. Jesse was clearly struggling from whatever they had gotten into the night before. Five empty bottles of wine on the table was probably a good indicator. "Guys...I fucking need sleep," he said. He grabbed one of the bottles that still had a little in it and took a deep drink. I told him the story, what James had said. He did not seem too concerned, but also was no longer angry with us.

"OK," he said. "I am going to get some sleep. We will talk about it when we get to the track today. We will work it out." Mare had already gone back to bed. "Sorry but I have a wicked fucking wine hangover." I felt better, but still was not convinced. I thought about texting Michael, but I did not want to interrupt his business. So Sophie and I had some breakfast and waited until it was time to go to the track. I was nervous when we got there. I looked to see if James was there, and the walk from the parking lot to the pavilion area -- where our table and bar were located -- seemed to take forever. I don't know what I was expecting, but I had the deep fear James and his two gruesome friends were going to pop up at any second.

It was a typically muggy day in Houston, where humidity is a way of life. It was mid-April now -- a few months after the debacle at the Shining Star -- and I had a court date coming up. It would probably get pushed back again. Paul had hooked me up with a lawyer friend, a guy who hung out at the track, but in the Jockey Club with the upper crust. His name was "Meteor" Murray. He did those goofy TV ads. But he was damned good. I suspected he would get the court date pushed back again and again, and eventually get the charges dropped. He had told me the farther we got from the incident, the better chance we would plead no contest and get deferred adjudication. Especially since Paul Sr. had paid the medical bills, made a substantial donation to the Star, and no one had any permanent damage. So I honestly had not even thought about it until today.

Low clouds hung in the air, and the humidity felt like a wet, 30-pound sack thrown over my shoulders. I kept thinking the Pavilion or those dirty brownish clouds might be the last thing I ever saw. But nothing happened. We entered into the Pavilion, which was all glass walls. It was located about the 16th pole of the track. It was a bad place to watch the live races, but it was a perfect place for simulcasting, with plenty of TVs, a bar right there and a table that was separate from everything else. It had been our home for a long time. I was starting to realize that was all coming to an end. Maybe we had been too greedy. I quietly blamed Jess. Before he was there, we were just a fun loving group. Now we were a target. I wasn't sure the money was worth it. But then, the disease...we all had it.

When Sophie and I walked in, almost everyone was there. Michael wasn't, but then I had not expected him. The notable absentees were the Pakis. They were almost always the first ones there. The sickness was returning to my stomach. Jesse and Mare were there, looking fresh as roses, nothing like the hungover duo we had seen that morning. Jesse came over and gave me a big hug. "Where are the Paks?" I asked. "Jr. has been texting them...no response. I suspect we will find out soon enough." Once again, the coyotes had picked on the weakest of the litter. That's what they did. When James and his two friends walked in, Jesse headed straight for them, Big Jim in tow. "I understand you want to talk to me," he said, getting well inside James' personal space.

James took a step back. There was none of the threatening man I had seen last night. I started to think James was a bully, picking on the weak.

I was the weak. The Paks were the weak. "We just want in on one big score," he said. "That's it." Jesse sighed, his eyes flashing brief anger. It was one of the few times I ever saw anything like that from him. Anger did not seem to be in his DNA. Jesse glared. "And if you had just asked me, I would have done it. I have no secrets. I will share with anyone who asks. Anyone who wants to know." James tried his best to look tough, but suddenly the scary old man was pretty scared himself. He really had not thought all this out. "I'm asking now," he said.

"No," Jesse said solemnly. "Fuck that. Not like this. You are blackmailing me. I don't do business that way." For a second, I saw some of Michael's confidence in Jesse. That Mafia-like coolness where nothing could touch him. "I think you need to tell me where my friends are." James tried to be cool himself, but it was already unraveling. Jesse could not be bullied. "Well, what would we know about that?" Jim noticed right away the Sam Houston duffle bag one of the other two was holding. It was what the DDs all used for cash. He said in his deep drawl, "that belongs to some friends of ours. And if I know 'em, there's $2,000 in there to play with today." It was easy to see why Jim was so good at his job. The threat of implied violence meant he never had to use it. Jim was the nuclear weapon of the group. He would always stay in the silo, never having to be used.

Jesse stepped in, smiling. "This isn't necessary," he said. "Give the bag to Jim, and bring us our friends, and we will forget all about this. And when you calm down, we will talk about letting you in on one. But it's not happening like this. Not ever. This is theft, pure and simple. I don't deal with that. Be better than this. Then we will talk." James had not considered they would be dismissed so easily. "We really need this money," he said. Now he was pleading. Jesse softened. "I get that. But it's not yours. You don't want to be this person. You aren't a thief. You are just a guy who needs a winner. And when this settles, we will talk. And I will give you one. Maybe one you will never forget. But until then, hand it over, give us our friends, and Big Jim here won't have to collect anything. I promise you we will talk in a couple weeks when everybody has calmed down."

James, to my surprise, did the right thing. He motioned to his friend to hand the bag over. He lowered his head, clearly beaten. He was not a bad man after all. He was just desperate. "We did not hurt them...we wouldn't. They are outside. I will go get them." Big Jim put a giant paw on the man's shoulder. "I will go with you." James nodded, and looked sheepishly at Jesse. "I'm sorry." Jesse lowered his head. "Don't apologize to me...You need to apologize to them..." James nodded again and left, Big Jim in tow. The other two were clearly not happy with the results. They went to the bar, where Spider bought them drinks and tried to distract them. But they were clearly pissed. James did not return, but Big Jim brought in the Paks, none the worse for wear. They hugged Jesse, and everybody else.

"Let's call it a day, gang," Jesse said. "Head to the Finish Line. Work this out." Everybody agreed, and we all went across the street. I texted Michael to let him know what had happened. His response was terse. "Back tonight. Finish Line. I have a plan." I showed it to Jesse, and he nodded. Jesse had already been working on that plan. "We should set up shop for a while here," he said. I will buy a satellite for the bar, and a few new TVs. We can watch the races here. We can get a bet runner. We will wait and see what Michael has in mind. It's not going to be just James and his friends anymore. If the tellers are talking...well, we can't hide this. It won't be just kidnapping. We will be getting robbed in the parking lot. Even with security. It's too dangerous."

Jesse was right. If the tellers - the people who took bets and cashed tickets - had been discussing our winnings, the entire track knew. A lot of desperate people. We had tipped the tellers well, but apparently it had not been enough. Jesse left, presumably to purchase what we needed. The rest of us sat quietly around a table just to the left of the oval bar. The Finish Line wasn't much, mostly wood, and would burn down if you left a match on the floor. There were banners of all the state's college football teams, plus LSU, Oklahoma and Oklahoma State. Huge Houston Texans, Astros and Rockets flags hung on the wall, with a picture of Secretariat winning the Belmont. The Finish Line called itself a sports bar, but it was really just a dive with a bunch of sports banners.

When Jesse returned, I noticed he pulled Sophie aside, and they were deep in conversation. That ugly emotion -- jealousy -- started to well. Especially when I saw how her face lit up. It was something I had never seen out of her, even with me. And then the emotional, angry me came out again. I really wish I could have controlled that. The whole scene reminded me this was all Jesse's fault. Stupidly huddling in a bar. Not able to go to our favorite place. This fucking con man had put us all in danger. Anger began to set in as well, and I was about to make a scene. But about then Michael walked in, looking as dapper as ever. He had a kid with him, no more than 23, 24 years old. The kid had moppy, long dark hair -- as if Enzo the baker's son had tried to go grunge. Sorry, are my movie references too much? That's how the kid looked. And I love movies.

Michael said his pleasantries, and introduced us. "Gang, this is Tony. You can call him Tickets. He's willing to run whatever bets from here for us for ten percent." My first reaction was no way, but Jesse nodded politely. "Can we trust him?" I asked. Michael shot me a look that made me instantly uncomfortable. Michael could do that. "This kid...he's my family. He's loyal. He's smart enough to avoid any of that nonsense from today. And if he gets pinched for being a ten percenter, he will take the heat." There were a lot ten percenters at the track. Before Jesse, we used them when we hit an IRS signer. They would cash the ticket for ten percent, so you would not have to declare taxes. That would be for the ten percenter to deal with. Every so often there would be a law enforcement sweep, and those guys would disappear. But new ones would pop up. Or the old ones would return. Michael was proposing this kid do that for all of our tickets. It made sense. He would make enough money that if anyone started digging he would look like a partner. And knowing Michael, this kid was probably protected and would not have to be worried about getting pinched anyway. "So that's the plan?" I asked, "We hide out here and let him make the bets?"

"It makes sense," Big Paul suddenly said. "We are safer here. We have alcohol. We will have TVs. And none of us will be at risk." I grudgingly had to admit it was a good plan. Still, Jesse sounded another alarm bell. "Derby's coming up in a few weeks. I think after that we get out of town for a while. Go to New Orleans. My treat. Stay there a couple weeks. Figure out our next move. Let all this cool down a little." By now, we all had enough money where we did not need to work. I could write from anywhere, and a couple weeks in the Big Easy would be fun. Again, he was making sense. I agreed, shot Sophie a glare, and decided to call it a night. It all fit together. As unhappy as I was, I had to agree it was a good plan. It was the first time Sophie and I had not slept in the same room since we had started seeing each other. But I wasn't interested, and did not even say goodbye. It was clear she did not care either. Something about that conversation with Jesse had fucked the whole thing up. It was funny how relationships could go. One minute you can't imagine being around anyone else. And then one misunderstanding, one weird look, and everything becomes murky. What's funny is I have been in the communications business my whole life. And I can't tell you how many times one conversation could have changed everything. Clear everything up. And so often we just fail to do it. We let our minds create the stories. And most of the time, we are completely wrong. I did not care about any of that. I got high, went home and passed out, starting to wish I had never met this asshole who was slowly ruining all of our lives.

BOOK NINE: THE GOSPEL ACCORDING TO LOUIS CHAPTER SIX

For two weeks, the Finish Line plan worked perfectly. Tickets handled everything, and with his ten percent was making a nice salary. He was a good kid, not real bright, but Michael was right about him. Completely loyal. I liked him. It wasn't the same though. It should have been. But there was something about the racetrack, the charm of its denizens, the fact that it had been our home away from home. Everybody had a story there. It was a microcosm of society, with the hyper rich rubbing elbows with people who could not afford a $2 bet.

The bar was OK. It was more private, and from a security perspective, it was significantly better. We had a back way out in a pinch, and the parking lot was easy to see from the windows. If anyone showed up, we could respond in a hurry. There was a small forest out back with a running trail where we could hide or get lost quickly. You would never walk that trail at night -- no telling who was out there -- but for hiding it would be perfect. When Tickets came and went, he was always followed by a black SUV. More friends of Michael's, I suspected. The kid seemed pretty safe.

Still, it was strange. Instead of sitting with us, Sophie felt the need to get us drinks and help Dave behind the bar. She and I had not been speaking much. She had texted a few times, but I had just told her I was tied up and would see her at the bar. She was always busy there, and I wasn't talking to her when she wasn't, so whatever had happened looked like it had ended as fast as it had started. I was OK with that. Better it dies fast than gets awkward.

Jesse came over to me and Michael and asked how we were doing. "Gotta say, Jess. This ain't the same," I said. "I have more than enough money. I just want to go back to having fun." Even Michael agreed. "Yeah this is OK, no question. But I miss the old days." Jesse nodded softly. "I understand." About then, Mare came over. She was looking better than ever, and even a little younger. She was glowing. Happy. Tonight -- after several re-starts -- was her last night at the Cup. "Gotta go, boys. One more run. Come and see me?" She had a way of getting to us, but that was her job. "Yeah," Michael said. "Might be fun." I laughed. "I'm in. Gotta help you say goodbye in style." I turned to Jesse. "Is that cool?"

He smiled. "Oh yeah. Might do us all some good." Tickets was now the keeper of the checks and cash, and he came in with the day's haul. It was substantial. Several of us had taken to giving him bonuses, which he refused at first, but after Michael -- who the kid called "Uncle Scraps," -- said it was OK, he took the money. Jesse, Michael and I went to the back patio, and Dave had just gotten me a wicked new shipment of Vancouver weed. It was potent. We were all alone out back, and Dave sure wasn't going to mind. So I lit up and offered them both. For the next hour, we got high as hell in relative silence. The weed was professional stuff, smuggled in from Canada. It was much better than the crap that had come across the border in Mexican asses that I had been getting by with for years. Just like anything in life. You make more money; you get better weed. For all the BS, the money had changed our lives for the better. For some it was flashy new cars. Some it was just comfort. For me, it was better weed.

We decided to walk over to the Cup, then burned a second one in the parking lot before we went in. Probably not a good idea. I was already in Zombieland before that. Jesse was reciting Plato and talking about the parable of the cave again. Michael just kept hugging us and saying "I would take a bullet for you guys." In his world, that was the greatest compliment. I damned sure wouldn't. Yeah, we were high as shit. We entered the Cup, with its long, neon entry way, paying the $10 cover charge. Inside, it was like every strip club in the world: dark, a little dirty, with private booths everywhere. We found a table near the side stage, where Mare was dancing. Her heart clearly wasn't into it, but she still looked sexy doing it. Michael found a girl named "Cinnamon" - a 20-something redhead, of course, and headed for the VIP room. It was $300 to get in, plus a bottle of champagne. Having done it a few times, it was another $200 to the girl to do whatever you wanted for an hour. I suspected Michael would spend the rest of the night in there.

As for me, the weed had kicked in fully. I had a drink nearby but could not touch it. It was like I was passed out, but wide awake and aware of everything in the room. My body just didn't respond. A few girls came by offering to dance, but all I could do was shake my head "no." Mare was off the stage, dancing for Jesse now. Several other girls were in the area, dancing for a wide array of wannabe gangsters, disgusting old men, and buff, well-built athletes who liked the atmosphere. There were two or three members of the Rockets, the local NBA team, who were here almost every night, whether they had a game or not. On game nights, they would be in late. On regular nights? They were here the whole time. The club didn't mind; it was good for business. The players would occasionally sign autographs, so they got discounts on dances. Even with all the money those guys made, they loved freebies.

I could feel the music. I don't know what song was playing, but the bass drum kept thumping in my throat, slowly. The dancers swayed, like cobras without any intent on pouncing. It was an oddly spiritual experience. The dancers' bodies melded with their clients, blurred images growing together. Then, they became swaying devils, with ghoulish red eyes that were somehow sexy. They whispered to me as they danced. I don't know what they said. It was comforting. I felt normal for the first time in a long time, and let my mind drift off and meld with the devil/cobra/dancers in a hellish mix that did not seem like hell at all. It was probably hours later when Jesse woke me out of my trance. I had no idea. Time had seemed to completely stop. Holy shit that was good weed.

"We got a problem," Jesse was saying, but the words seemed to take minutes to come out. "We need to get outta here, Lou." Sophie had arrived at some point and was huddled next to Mare, who was dressed to leave, no longer in her stripper gear. Michael and Cinnamon were there as well. The DJ was cheerfully announcing last call. Meanwhile at the bar, James, his two friends and a few more reprobates we recognized from the track were watching us. And they had devil eyes. Only these did not comfort me. "Let go to Mare's," Jesse said. I think we left. I downed the drink that had been sitting there for hours, but I don't remember getting to Mare's place, don't remember drinking like a fish when I got there. I just remembered those dancing devils. How they comforted me so. How I belonged with them. Until I finally woke up the next morning.

Waking up after overdoing it on weed is much better than waking up hung over. With a hangover, your eyes are a mess, your head hurts, your body hurts. Your stomach feels like you swallowed a turd. With weed you wake up fresh as a daisy. I was apparently the first one awake. I was on the floor. Michael and Cinnamon were naked on the couch next to me. Through the open bedroom door, I could see Jesse, Mare and Sophie all curled up naked as well. Jesse appeared to be staring at me with one open eye. At first I wasn't sure how to feel. I would have wanted an easy out at some point. This would have been it. But at the same time, I was angry. Jesse had taken everything that mattered. My life at the table. My status as the leader. And now, the first girl I had actually liked in a while. The money wasn't worth it. OK, that's a lie. The money was everything.

I did a quick check, making sure I had my phone, wallet and keys, and quietly left through the front door. Mare's place was only about a half mile from mine, so I walked, quietly steaming. It had occurred to me I was completely sick of Jesse's shit. I began to formulate a plan. I would do Derby Day. I would do New Orleans. But then I was pulling up stakes. Dallas maybe. Spend my time at Lone Star, make new friends. After all, the magazine did not care where I lived. I just had to produce. And then it hit me. I had a story due today. Fuck.

I got home, grabbed my notes, and knocked it out in a couple hours and sent it in. It was about Ecstasy making a comeback with teenagers, centered on a kid who had overdone it and decided to climb on oil pump in a field. He had fallen to his death, and his parents blamed the outbreak of Ecstasy. It has always been there, but lately it had gone epidemic again. I passed out after I finished the story and decided to spend a couple days alone, waiting to hear back from my editor. She called the next morning and said she loved it, but had a couple minor questions, which we cleared up. Her name was Jennifer. She was extremely smart, a former intern of mine. The ex-wife had caught us fucking in our garage, which is why I got kicked out of the house. I had thought Jen might be the one to replace the last one, but she hated gambling and drinking. It was too bad. She fucked like a champ. I thought about that every time we talked. So I got high again and fell asleep, and did not plan on going back to the Finish Line until Saturday. Derby Day. It was Monday.

The plan worked, but each day I had to answer a dozen texts about where I was. I kept telling everyone I had a piece to finish and would be there Saturday. By Thursday, the texts were about how much money I had waiting for me. Except for Sophie's, of course. Hers seemed desperate. She kept asking to come by, saying she really needed to talk to me. I answered the first couple with the standard "really busy, will talk soon."

By Friday she had given up. Meteor hadn't, however. Big Jim and I had a hearing on the Shining Star mess that day. He was confident but warned me to be prepared for the worst. It was the first Kentucky Oaks day I had missed at the track in years. I did not realize at the time I would never see that race again.

BOOK 10: THE GOSPEL ACCORDING TO MICHAEL CHAPTER FOUR

I pulled into the parking area of a large cabin on Crystal Beach. I had been here many times before, sometimes just taking a weekend for myself. It had been a few years, but Frankie had once thrown lavish parties here. Since the heart attack, he had stopped. That was all he had stopped, though. When I left my old friend, I was worried sick. Frankie had left himself go. This would not end well. It was the least I could do to take care of Frankie's son. My godson.

Crystal Beach was still being rebuilt after Hurricane Ike. Frankie's place was one of the few that had still been standing after the storm blasted though. Crystal Beach was a playground for oil and gas weekenders from Beaumont, primarily. And while they called them "cabins," most were four or five bedroom weekend homes, and Frankie's stood out among those. The island had been a ghost town for months, but was starting to come back to life. Houses were being rebuilt. Stores were re-opening. But the area was still in comeback mode, and there were not many people there. It was perfect for what I needed to do.

It had only taken a month to repair Frankie's place, mostly because he had his own construction company and they dropped everything to get it repaired. Many of the other sites were still being cleaned up. Part of it still looked like an A-bomb had been dropped on the place. Ike was a terrible storm. I remember being huddled in my place, waiting to lose electricity, watching the news reports. A TV reporter, no more than 22, was on the Galveston Seawall. This idiot always got in the water during a storm to show how deep it had gotten. But this time, that would have been suicide. Massive waves crashed over the seawall, bringing debris with them. The girl reporter sounded sad in saying that we were looking at the remains of what had been the Galveston Hooters and a "bar nearby." Fucking amateur. The "bar nearby" was the Balinese Room, one of the most historical places in Galveston. It had been a huge casino at one point. Bing Crosby hung out there. In recent years it had been a combo bar/museum, a tip of the cap to the city's mafia past, when the Maceo family ran it all. I had spent many nights there. And now it was gone.

But it was just a "bar nearby" to some 20-something idiot. Oh well. That's TV. She was hired for her looks. The station had kind of failed on that front, too. Regardless, Galveston took a beating.

Crystal Beach, a ferry ride from the Island, got it much worse. The aftermath was ugly. Animals went insane because there was no fresh water, and even cows became dangerous. Alligators became vicious, aggressive predators. People were not let on the peninsula for weeks. By the time it had been cleaned up, it was well into 2009. The area still looked like a meteor had crashed from space and taken out almost everything for miles. Frankie's place was one of the few up and running that April. It made a perfect hideout for a couple of would-be criminals.

One of them answered the door, long, curly black hair covering his eyes. He was tall, lanky, and had grown out a beard that made him look like what we would have called a "beatnik" in my day. But the handsome facial features were no mistake. Frankie Jr. looked like a thin version of his old man.

He pushed the hair from his blue eyes and his face lit up a little, even as he tried to act like he didn't care. "Uncle Scraps…" He then went into full cool kid mode. "Dad sent you, did he? Wasted your trip."

I smiled, and before he could react I gave him a big hug. He didn't seem to mind. "Missed you, kid. You look good." I was lying. He looked like he hadn't slept. He was wearing a torn Shinedown concert shirt, old swim trunks and really ugly flip flops. But he was still a damned good looking kid.

"I know you don't want to see anybody, but my old ass drove all the way down here. And I haven't seen you in years. Take a walk with your godfather?" I asked. I had not seen him in three years, to be exact, since his 18th birthday. He didn't look much different, but he might have shot up another inch or two. He was taller than me. He snuck a quick glance over his shoulder inside, nodded, and closed the door. We walked in silence for a while, listening to the bang bang of construction, eventually talking about the damage Ike had done. Small talk. We got caught up, and the kid admitted he wished his "uncle" had been around more.

There was always something about the beach down here. The water was brown, due to the ship channel. More often than not, the beach was covered in seaweed. But there was something about the power of the waves as they licked the beach. It was something bigger than me. I loved it, as dirty as that beach was. I knew Louis did too. The kid seemed to be mesmerized as well. That water was something. And in the case of Ike, it had been downright dangerous. Most normal days, its beauty and power still hid sharks, riptides, all sorts of things that could ruin your day in a hurry. And yet being next to it was comforting. Even after the storm, the place had a charm. Crystal Beach would come back. It would always come back. "Doing any writing?" I asked.

He had been waiting for the small talk to end. "Uncle Scraps...dad wants me to be a writer. It's not for me." I was playing the uncle role to the hilt. "Kid, you got into the Creative Writing program at UH. That's big stuff. That's write your ticket stuff." He laughed. "Dad could always write my ticket anyway. It didn't matter what I wound up doing." I let the waves wash up on our feet in silence for a few minutes as we wandered along the beach. "I wish I could write. I really do. Much better than what I do for a living. But I get it. And you know what? Kid, you got in that school on your own. You did that. Your dad had nothing to do with it. That was all you." More silence. The water was cold on my bare feet as I walked with shoes in hand.

"So what do you want?" I asked him. "Tell me. I will work with your dad and make it happen. That's what I do." This seemed to get through to him. He knew of all the people in the world who could have an influence on his dad, the number one guy was standing on this beach with him. He looked down at the sand, kicking a crab away. "I want to take over the business when dad is gone," he said. "My family has been building it for years. I want to be a part of it. Ernesto has some great ideas…"

It was funny. I could tell his heart really wasn't in that idea. This was just a kid that needed to be part of his family. No mom. A dad who was hardly around. He was way too sensitive to ever survive doing what we did. This Ernesto thing was an excuse. "Ernesto? The kid staying with you?" He nodded yes. "The one who stole one of your dad's shipments?" Jr. looked like he had been punched in the gut. "No…"

"That truck job he told you about? That was your dad's." Frankie Jr. was forlorn now. And I knew I had him. "You didn't know? Of course you didn't. No way you hang out with that guy, let him in your dad's place if you knew he stole from your family." I paused for a while. He was just standing there with that mopey look. "It's hard to trust people, kid. I don't trust too many people. They will always let you down." I let things sink in. "Is dad mad at me? Am I in trouble?" He seemed genuinely concerned. He would never cross his dad, even to get his attention. The kid was every bit as good as I thought he was. "Of course not, I said. But if you really want in, you know what you have to do, right? Kid has to be taught a lesson…"

Now Frankie Jr. was almost pale white. Sick to his stomach.

"Uncle Scraps…I didn't know…I don't…" He was stammering now. Trying to make sense of it. A perfect time for me to pounce. But even then, I knew I had to show him. "Kid, let me tell you what I think. This life isn't for you. I don't think you want it. You just miss having a family.

You miss your dad. I get that. You and your dad are about all I have. Everything else I left in New York. Ever tell you I had a brother?" He stared at the sun beaming over the water, and shook his head softly.

"He died in Jr. High. My parents couldn't handle it. Split up. My dad was killed over something stupid. My mom OD'd. Your grandfather looked out for me. Your dad was like a brother…." My voice trailed off. "There's nothing like having family, son. Sometimes they don't realize what they mean to us. They need to be reminded. Your dad needed to be reminded, but you are all that matters to him." He lightened the mood. "Well, it sure looks like I am going to wind up with a little brother or sister if he keeps banging that blonde." We both laughed. "Yeah," I said. "I found out yesterday I'm supposed to be the best man. You fucking kidding me?"

He was comfortable now. And he was paying attention. "Listen kid, your dad...me...we did what we had to do so you didn't have to. He's almost completely legitimate now. This restaurant chain he started is going national. The shipping is legal. The other stuff is turning into peanuts. The whole game is changing. In ten years, you will just be collecting checks from businesses you own that are being run by corporate dickweeds. This life you seek? It won't exist."

The kid was smart. He already knew all this, and now he wanted a way out of the Ernesto mess. But he also was in love with Ernesto's sister. This, of course, complicated things. "You are right, Uncle Scraps." He did not sound convinced. "But how do I clean this up? I really like Anita, and if something happens to Ernesto…Their family is really,

really close." We started walking back to the cabin. A black SUV was parked behind my Cadillac with two men waiting inside. They had everything I needed to prove a point. "So what are you going to do about Ernesto?" He asked. He was starting to sound a little panicked. "I don't want to screw this up."

I laughed, and the old me was coming back. "Tell you what, kid, you let me handle this. You watch. If you still want in after I'm done, I will work it out with your dad. But when I am finished, your little friend Ernesto is going to leave the country, and he won't come near you or his sister again. And he damned sure won't tell her it's your fault." The kid's eyes lit up. "How are you going to pull that off?" I smiled. The plan had been swirling in my head since I had left Frankie Sr. "First you need to put some makeup on. See the guys in the back of that SUV...then do a little acting. They will coach you. I will take it from there, OK?"

The kid smiled. "If you are trying to convince me this isn't fun, you are doing a bad job." A dark cloud crossed my face, and he noticed it immediately. "Hold judgement on the fun part. This? Yeah, this is fun. But wait until you see the other side of it."

I waited a half hour, then the two men in the truck slipped into the garage, carrying boxes. One of them gave me a thumbs up, so I went and opened the door. A Hispanic kid, no more than 160 pounds, was standing in the kitchen. He was wearing only swim trucks, cornrowed black hair and had an angel tattooed across his chest. Typical punk. "Who the fuck are you, man?" he asked. He grabbed a knife and held it menacingly. "I should ask you," I said. "This is my friend's place. He gave it to me for the week." I slid my jacket open, making sure the kid could see the handle of my Glock tucked into my pants.

"Well I'm already here," the kid said. "So get the fuck out, you fucking fossil." He stepped toward me in what appeared to be a threatening fashion, but I knew it was just show. I started to walk away, slowly, knowing he would approach me from behind and keep talking crap. As soon as he did, I spun around him, got him in a headlock, and buried his face in an ether covered rag. He fought for about 45 seconds before going limp. Yes, I was old school. I loved using ether for jobs like this. You had to be careful not to touch any of it yourself, and always wear gloves. I had seen it backfire many times. But not today. Had to give him credit. Tough kid after all. He was strong for his size, and he fought the ether hard. Then again, little fucker called me a fossil. And maybe I was. But today, I was Scraps. I was one of the most feared men on the East Coast. And Ernesto was about to get an old school lesson. Sometimes in life, you have those moments where you realize what you were supposed to be. This was one of my moments. When Ernesto finally woke up, everything was set up for my act.

The guys had soundproofed the massive garage. Ernesto was handcuffed to a chair in front of a giant backdrop, the kind golf stores used to let people test clubs. I had set up a plastic tee on astroturf, about 15 feet from Ernesto. Jr. was also in a chair, tied up, slumped over in a corner. "What the fuck?" Ernesto said. His groggy mind was trying to process everything. I walked over, golf club in hand, and got inches from his face. "So you are Ernesto..." Ernesto began cussing me, dropping

113

every imaginable threat. I motioned to one of the men, who put a gag on him. "That's better," I said. Ernesto just kept trying to yell, but it came out as "mmmmm!" "MMMMM!"

I smiled and pulled a chair close to him as he struggled against his bindings. "So let me talk for a minute, and maybe you walk out of here…" He tried to spit at me, and finally calmed down when he realized he was spitting on himself. I motioned to Jr., and the other man pulled the kid's head up, revealing a fractured face. "So that kid tells me he stole from his dad. And with all due respect, you think he looks bad now…" Again, Ernesto started cursing, but again it came out as muffled gibberish. "He says he pulled the job with hired hands, doesn't have the money, and you know nothing about it. Ernesto began nodding feverishly, as if that were true...I think he was trying to say "that's right, motherfucker," but it came out as "mmmmriighhaaa er."

I smiled, fatherly. Oh man, I had missed this. Knowing you had someone. Knowing whatever bleak future this fucker had was in my control. It was like we were the only two people in the world. Like we were dancing on the beach. "But you know what I think?" The kid shook his head side to side, viciously. "I think he's lying." Now he was squirming again. I walked around, picking up a golf club, and sat back down, the head of the club an inch from Ernesto's face. "I think he knows how to keep his mouth shut. I think he likes your sister. Gotta give him credit. Kid took a beating and never wavered. Look at that face…" Frankie appeared to be passed out. "Now...that's my godson. I took no pleasure in it. And you see what I did to him, right?"

114

Now the kid was really squirming, nervous, his eyes bulging, trying to scream "no" through the gag. It came out as "ooo! OOO!" I loved this part. The realization. The kid understanding just what I was capable of doing to him. "You'll get your chance to talk," I said. "Let me tell you what I think is going on here. So I think YOU pulled this job. The kid didn't know but tried to protect you because of your sister. You have his dad's money. And if that's the case, and you return it, I might let you live. And if Frankie was telling the truth...well I am going to punish you a little anyway, because that shit is fun to me."

Again he was screaming. I walked over to an old school boom box/cd player I had brought, and punched the button. "I hope you like music." The opening strains of Drowning Pool's "Bodies" began to play. "I know it's loud," I said, "but the neighbors won't hear a thing." I walked over to the golf bag, placed a ball on the tee, and began speaking, matter of factly. "Now I am no great golfer. Bad slice. But I used to enjoy the game. Nice practice setup we have here. I like to start with a club that's not hard to hit for my warmups, like a five- iron." I addressed the ball, took a swing, and it whizzed past Ernesto's cheek before hitting the backdrop with a loud "WHACK."

"If you warm up with a pitching wedge first, you slow your swing down, but you get a false sense of security, so I like the five... More honest, because it's a full swing." Another shot. This one caught Ernesto on the right arm with a loud "CRACK." The arm turned instantly purple. He screamed in pain. I just kept talking. "Plus, at this range, a five iron is going to catch you below the neck, unless I hit behind it and get under it…" The third shot hit him in the face. Teeth exploded. "Like that one. Sorry, I'm out of practice." The next shot shattered ribs on Ernesto's left side. Now he was clearly crying…I thought he was trying to say "I'll talk," but between the gag and the shattered jaw, it was coming out as "mmwwalk."

"Now I try a driver. Now this will do some real damage. And I am a badass with a driver." Man I was having fun. I pulled out the big club. I had no intention of using it. If I hit him in the right spot with a flush swing of the driver, I could kill him. I motioned to one of the men, who removed the gag. "Pleashe…" he said, blooding pouring from his mouth. "I'll tell you the truhhh…"

"I don't know," I said. "The kid over here made it to the driver. I think I should take at least one swing." And then he completely crumpled. "NO!" He admitted he had done it, had not told Frankie and hoped that something like that would get Frankie to let him in with his dad. Maybe he would find the money, pin it on somebody else and Frankie's dad would respect him. Nobody was supposed to know it was him. He had spent some of the money but the rest was under the bed and God please no more and don't kill him. I sent one of the men upstairs and stopped the music. "Under the bed? Fucking amateur." When he brought the bag down, it was about $20,000 short of the worth of the shipment. "You are a little light, kid…" There was some pretty good weed, though, that I thought Louis might enjoy. "Pleashe…I'll make it back…"

"No, you won't," I said, his eyes getting huge. "You are a dumb fucking kid. And it's a bad investment letting you live. But Frankie here

116

took a beating for you, so that earns you a little bit of a pass." I pulled another $20k out of the bag. "Carmo here is going to patch you up. You are going to take this money and get the fuck out of America. That kid over there earned you this. If you are still here in three days, or we see you alive anywhere in this country, you are a dead man. You get that?"

"Pleashe...my family is here."

"Yeah," I said. "And we know who they are. If you want them to stay alive, you will get as far away from them as possible. Get dead to them. And you ever come around the kid over there again, his dad will kill you both. Clear enough?" He tried to protest for a while, but I just stared at him, my iciest look, and he knew there were no negotiations. And in the end, he knew he got off light. I turned to Carmo. "Clean him up, and clean this place up. Make sure he gets across the border. I don't care if he's from Mexico or not." I turned to the other man. I had never really gotten his name. "Take the other one to my car. I'm taking him to his dad."

I gave one, last long look at Ernesto. "You are a lucky man, kid. Don't waste this second chance." He was loudly sobbing now. I wasn't sure he heard me. I did not care. The kid would never be back. And I was pretty sure I had accomplished all my goals. I wasn't completely sure right away, because Jr. spent the first 45 minutes of the trip wiping off makeup. We sat in silence otherwise. It was normally about an hour and 15 minutes taking I-10 going through Winnie, but traffic was bad today. When I finally spoke, he interrupted me right away. "That was terrible, Uncle Scraps. You were enjoying it, weren't you? That's sick, man.

117

Really sick." I nodded, with a wry smile. "That's what you guys do? I mean, he had it coming, but still...You scared the fuck out of me, man." I laughed. "Somebody has to be the one to deal with it," I said. "You don't want to do that. I know you don't. It was all you could do to not throw up when you saw that ball shatter his jaw. You don't ever want to do that."

"No," he said softly. "I don't. Thanks, Uncle Scraps. For everything. You were right. This isn't for me." I smiled at him. I had missed a lot in life. Being a father. Having a family. For once, I felt like the kid's real uncle, the one who bailed him out of a jam, the one who put him back on his right path. "Don't worry about it, kid. That's what family is for. Just do your old uncle a favor and get back to school, OK?" He nodded, then smiled slyly. "Hey...can I write about this?" We had a good laugh. "Just change the names, kid." About a half hour later we pulled into Frankie Sr.'s place. Frankie Jr. couldn't wait to tell his dad the whole story as we all had drinks. Sr. just smiled. "I still should have killed his ass," he laughed. "Getting soft in my old age."

"You might still get your chance." I said, and tossed him the bag of money. "I covered the kid's end. A gift for my godson in case it works out with this girl." Frankie glared at me. "Scraps...you know damned well I'm not taking your money for that piece of shit."

"Fuck you, Frankie. Not your call." He laughed. He really did want out of the life, too. I could see that. Maybe this girl was good for him. Maybe this whole incident would get him and Jr. closer together. I really believed it would. I gave him a hug, him and the kid both. Man this felt different. After all these years, I truly felt at home. But I knew my other home was shaky at the moment, and just like that, I had to shift into a different gear. "I gotta get to the bar," I said. Shit's getting dicey."

"Yeah," Frankie agreed. "I got eyes on it. All good. Pick up Vinny Jack's kid on the way. He's expecting you. Lives in Meyerland so a little out of the way. Jewish mom, wouldn't you know? Kid's not real bright, but he's good with money, loyal as shit and he worships you. I will have a couple boys on lookout. Former military. Iraq and Afghanistan. Paying them very well so you guys should be safe at that bar." Frankie Jr. came up, looked me in the eyes and started bawling. "Thanks, uncle. Thanks for everything." I realized at that point how much I loved this kid. And his father. My eyes welled up a little too.

"Anytime, kid. And you already thanked me."

He pulled away, composed and embarrassed. "It better not be another three years before I see you again." I laughed. I was doing that a lot lately. "Hell no. I will surprise at campus one day. You got a lot of redheads there? They could use an old man to teach them a trick or three." Frankie Jr. laughed, and we shared another drink as I looked at his dad, who nodded at me knowingly and mouthed a quick "thank you." I was pretty sure he followed that with "I love you, brother."

I smiled, nodded, and left, almost forgetting to return the golf clubs. Then I went to pick up our new bet runner. I had the weird, desperate feeling I would never see either Frankie again, the only two people on the planet who I knew I truly loved. And it took a session practicing golf to make me realize it. Who was I kidding? I felt the same way about my track group. And now they needed me. Frankie and Frankie were going to be OK. And Scraps was back. Dangerous, cunning Scraps, ready to take on the people who had threatened that other family.

BOOK 11: THE GOSPEL ACCORDING TO LOUIS CHAPTER SEVEN

So we sat outside the courtroom, Big Jim, me and Spider, who was there to support Jim. Pete's and Jr.'s cases had been dismissed, but the two of us were still trying to get clear. Figures. Me and the black guy taking the heat. That's America for you. Meteor had been in the judge's chamber, arguing a point of law. We were stuck outside, waiting. I couldn't do time. Not for Jesse. Not for that son of a bitch.

Passing the time while waiting for the gallows is the hardest thing in the world. It had already been hanging there for months, but being in the court room really hammered it home to me. So I did what I always tried to do. Interview people. Get the real story. We had talked many times before, but I had never really known why Spider and Jim were so close. I started by asking them what they were planning to do with their money.

"Buy myself an old-fashioned jailbreak," Jim drawled. We laughed. "Naw," he said. "I want to move back to Beaumont and buy my old man's catfish farm back. Family sold it after he passed. That's my home. I want it back. And after tomorrow I should have more than enough." Spider smiled, like a proud father. "Bagel shop," he said. "Like in New York. Fuck these kolaches. And I want out of the book business. Dirty shit. Besides, everyone is going online to bet these days anyway. Only a matter of time until it ends." They asked me, and I told the truth. "I don't have a clue. I'm just waiting to lose it all again." They laughed, and I asked Spider how the two had hooked up.

He paused for several seconds. "I guess we've gotten to be friends, huh, Louis?" I smiled. "Yeah, I hope so. I sure think so." He turned serious. "OK, but this is just for you. Don't write it." I lied to his face. "Of course not." He sighed. "Business partner of mine tried to shave points at a game. It never happened, because word got out, and three kids were suspended and eventually kicked out of school. Pissed me off. I might be a sonofabitch, but I don't need to be a part of shaving. Bad business. "So I quit partnering with the guy right after. I know what's up, but the school never announces why the kids were kicked out. Turns out they found about $5,000 on each of them. My partner had paid two of the kids; I knew that. Big Jim had been saving his money for three years waiting tables to help his dad keep his catfish farm. He lost his scholarship, his job, and his money. He had nothing to do with any of it. But it was easiest just to cut all three loose rather than take a chance. And poor Jim here...he was just a big old country kid, honest as they come, word is his bond. Just assumes if he tells the truth he will be OK."

Jim lowered his head. "They didn't listen, even when the other two insisted I wasn't in on it. Hell, I was a second string linebacker. What could I have done? Would have been a starter the next year..." His voice trailed off. Spider jumped back in. "Eventually my partner flees the country, and nothing can be proved and no charges are filed. But that doesn't mean Jim gets his scholarship or his life back." Jim smiled. "Spider here, he comes to see me, pays me my money back and offers

122

me a job. All I have to do is stand there and look dumb. And we've been together ever since." A hint of sadness came over Spider's face. "It was too late to save the farm. Kid could have been a borderline NFL talent. We'll never know. Greedy fucking idiot ruined his life." I was truly touched. "You are a better man than me, Spider." He laughed. "Alan. Alan Silver. How long have you known me? And I've always been Spider?"

"Well, I knew a little...Silver's Kolaches is kind of a dead giveaway." He laughed. "But, no, I didn't know your first name was Alan," I said. "No offense, but I like that better." He returned the smile. "Me too." Even Big Jim seemed surprised. "Well, aw still like Spider..." I brought up a topic that had been hanging in the air for everybody. "Guys, how much more of this do we need? I like this New Orleans plan and all, but do we really need to keep going? Isn't it time to quit?" Alan laughed. "We can't quit. You know that. We are going to ride this thing into the ground until somebody kills us or Jesse leaves. The sickness, man." I hated the answer, but deep down I knew it was right. Meteor came back out, hair slicked back, wearing a pinstripe suit and carrying a briefcase. He looked us both over. "Good news, bad news, boys."

We stood up, eager. "Jim, charges are dropped. Free and clear. Yes, I am a fucking great lawyer. Don't say a word, I know." Jim tried to speak, but I interrupted. My heart sank. "I'm the bad news." Meteor sighed. "I'm still going to win this. But we go to trial next month. The woman who worked there claims you hit her and won't drop it." "The lying bitch!" I snapped. "She fucking hit ME! I'm a coward. I didn't hit anybody. Well, that mouse lady maybe, but…" "Don't admit to that!" He snapped. "Could have been anybody. I believe you did not strike Ms. Johnson. But it's your word against hers and she wants someone to pay. So we are going to have to prep hard for this. I can plea you out, but not without doing time…"

"No," I snapped. "No time. I'll take my chances." Meteor looked me over. "That's what I think you should do. I think we can win. I am a great fucking lawyer. I will discredit her. Just stay out of trouble until then, OK?" I nodded, and just like that, the Type-A, brash lawyer was off to make another deal. Jim looked at me, sullenly. "Don't worry, Lou. I will testify. I saw you cowering in the corner." I tried to laugh. "Appreciate that, big fella. Let's get a drink." They hit the bar, collecting their Oaks Day winnings. As usual, it was a big day. Sophie tried to corner me, but I waved her off. "I can't talk right now. I'm trying to think of a way to stay out of fucking jail." Jesse wandered over, and brought me a drink. "Hey man...talk to the girl, OK? And forget about this shit. It's gonna be fine." I snapped. "Fine? FINE? I am going to wind up in jail because of some lying bitch when I never should have been there in the first fucking place. Damn you Jesse! Why did you have to fuck everything up?" I stormed out, having no idea what would come next. Or what should come next.

I had a text from Jen asking if I could come by the office. I decided anything was better than being around here. So I hopped in my car and headed for downtown Houston. The traffic on 290 was as bad as always, so at least it gave me time to sober up and start making plans. I would do

Derby Day tomorrow, but I was going to pass on New Orleans. Dallas, maybe? Just come back for the trial. Never see these people again. Start the new group at Lone Star Park. It was a good plan. It was time to get as far away from Jesse as possible. And in the back of my mind, Sophie, too. That had played out. Parking sucked downtown, and it was going to get a lot worse. New bars were cropping up everywhere, and new apartments were being built. Downtown had always been dead during the evening, but all that was changing. Houston was extremely spread out -- not unlike LA -- but its center was slowly becoming a true downtown. In ten years, it would be crawling with people. It wasn't there yet, but it was getting there. I found a place to park for $6 and went to the office, an old, two story brick building that looked out of place among a group of newly built skyscrapers. That was one of the weird things about downtown; you would have these ridiculously old, antique buildings right next door to massive, shiny new oil money buildings.

The magazine did not need many offices. There were four fulltime editors, a receptionist, and the man who owned the company. He really did not do anything, but he liked being there and looking important. The writers almost never came in. There was no need. I flirted with the receptionist, a new girl who could not have been more than 20, but she was extremely attractive. I got the sense she wasn't into fossil fucking, though, because she ignored me with ease and sent me to Jen's office. Jen was 29 years old, short -- no more than 5'1" -- but very beautiful. Her dad was from Egypt, and she had his dark skin and eyes. She also had a massive rack that you could not help but notice. When she was an

125

intern years ago, we had called her short stack. She smiled and gave me a huge hug, and it was almost all breast. Man, we had some great times. My marriage was basically over when we started hooking up. We were working at the newspaper then, and we would go out after work, drink, and fuck in one of our cars. Later, when she got hired by the magazine, she got a place downtown, and we spent lot of time there. It was stupid how we got caught. Paula was having a party for her law firm buddies and some of my journalist friends. Jen and I got drunk and snuck into the garage. If we had been sober, we would have been done long before Paula walked in on us.

It's funny. I would have married Jen. But the gambling scared her off. Her dad had a huge problem with it, and she had seen the disease up close and personal. It had been almost five years since our garage fucking days, and she had added a few pounds, but nothing that took away from her beauty. Even her breasts seemed bigger. "So, we need to talk…" she said. Those conversations never ended well. "Sure," I said, "but don't let me forget. I have a gift for you in the car." She smiled, head down, with that slightly shy, demure look that always turned me on. "Lou, we have layoffs coming here. It's not going to be for a couple months, but you know how the print business is these days."

The words hung there for a minute, and my first thought was strange. It wasn't about me. It was about her. "You are OK, right?" I asked. She smiled. I think she was surprised that I asked about her first. I decided right then and there I was going home with her tonight. I knew how to play her. It was going to happen. "Of course," she said. "We aren't going

126

to lay off any editors. But we are going to go freelance for most of the writing now. Which means no more fulltime writers…" I had been expecting this for a while. They were wasting money paying eight of us to write once a month, sometimes less.

"Obviously we will want to use you as a freelancer. You are our most popular writer. But it's going to be competitive. The Chronicle just laid off a bunch of good people, too. I just wanted to give you time to make plans." It was funny. I did not feel bad at all. It was kind of like when Paula had caught us; I wanted to get caught. I wanted out. This job had become the same way. I did not need it anymore, and was ready for something new. The only real issue would be health insurance, and the kids were on mine. I would have to sort that out. Otherwise, I was relieved. "Talk to me…" she said softly. I smiled. "Have a drink with me. I have a lot to tell you." She shook her head. "I'm sort of seeing someone, Lou…" That was her go-to line. It meant she had been on a blind date or met someone online and been out once or twice. It was her arm's-length reaction. I knew it well. It had not stopped us from hooking up a couple times, but it had been a few years.

"Not like that," I said. "Let's celebrate us working together for this long. It's been a great ride." She seemed confused. "You aren't upset?" The smile on my face was genuine. "No, not even a little. Listen, Jen, our business is dying. You know it. A year from now it might be you on this side of the table. I'm still young enough that I can do something else. And it is time. Maybe finish the novel. Maybe just become a hermit somewhere for a while. There's that great line in Fight Club -- 'It's only when you've lost everything that you are free to do anything.' That's how I feel. My future is wide open." She smiled, and I knew I was getting to her. "Jesus, Lou, you've changed a lot."

She had no idea. At the time, I had no idea, either. "Yeah, well, old age and wisdom and that kind of shit..." She smiled grimly and got back to the task at hand. "Well, I will let you know when it actually happens. My guess would be July first, start of the next quarter. There will be a severance package..." I interrupted. "Forget all that for now. You did your job. Can we go get a drink?" She smiled. "Yeah. I would like that." The Lone Star Saloon was an absolute armpit. It made no sense that someone as classy as Jen would love coming here. It was old, dirty, and right across the street from a bus station. The homeless would come in and hit you up right at the bar. The rest rooms were locked to keep them out, and you had to get the bartender to buzz you in if you needed to pee. The drinks were overpriced, the service sucked. And yet Jen loved it here. I think it was her way of slumming it.

The only other people in the place besides the bartender were two Pay Per Views in the corner. (I'm sorry, Pay Per Views are hookers. Should have mentioned that). They were easy to spot. Skirts too small, big, heeled boots, tight tops, too much makeup. They were arguing. Apparently their appointments had not made it. They were all over downtown, and you had to be sure they were actually women if you were going to partake. I had learned to spot them from an old friend in Vegas. He created a game called spot the Pay Per View. Whoever spotted the

128

most in an hour won $100 from the other guy. I got damned good at it, and this was an easy two points.

We slowly sipped our Jack and Cokes, and Jen made small talk, asking me if I had seen Paula and the kids lately (no, she keeps them away from me), had I talked to any of our old running buddies (no, they never liked me anyway, especially when I stole Jen from all of them), was I still gambling. I gave that slight, sly, smile. This is where I closed the deal for the night. "I've got Derby Day tomorrow with some friends, but no, I am pretty much done with gambling." Her face turned dark. I had struck a major nerve. "Now, Louis? Now? I'm 29 years old. If I ever want to get married at this point, I am going to have to settle for somebody. Do you know how few good people are out there at my age? How many smart ones? Funny ones? Guys you could spend time with and enjoy being with? Why couldn't you do that when I was 24? We could have been great together. I asked for one thing from you…One thing…" I ordered a couple shots and another round of drinks. I put my hand softly on her shoulder. "You know that was too much to ask. And it was too much for me to ask you to ride it out. And 29…come on girl. You are the total package, and you know it. And you can pick and choose."

"No," she said. "I can't. Everyone my age is an ass hole. I have no plan for the rest of my life." I laughed. "Man, 29…you are just getting started…I'm 43 and just getting started." She softened again, the alcohol starting to kick in "You really are quitting?" I lied. "Yeah, think so. I don't need the money anymore. I came into a bunch recently. Enough to never have to work again, if that's what I want. So I don't really need to gamble." Man, I was convincing. Just like at the poker table. The perfect bluff. "That's really awesome, Lou."

"It's liberating," I said. "Hey, let's finish these, and I want to give you your gift. I probably need to get on the road soon anyway." Her reaction to that told me everything I needed to know; she was all- in. It had been too easy. When we got to the car, I pulled a duffle bag out of the trunk with that day's winnings. "I want you to have this," I said. "An apology for costing you five years. A thank you for always looking out for me. And just something nice for one of the few people I have ever really cared about." She looked in the bag, her eyes wide. "Louis, how much is this?" She immediately looked around the empty parking lot to see if anyone else was there. It probably wasn't smart to have that kind of money out in this part of downtown, but it was the capper to my plan. And it was much safer than that bar. "About $20,000. I told you I had a lot of money now. Buy yourself a place down here. Get a better apartment. Go shopping at the Galleria. Put it in savings. I don't care. It's a gift. Do whatever you want with it." She hugged me again, and man, those breasts. Although I thought I could actually feel the giant mole on the right one. Why had she never taken care of that? It was the one blemish on a damned near perfect package. She kissed me lightly on the cheek. "Will you walk me home? With this kind of money, I'm a little nervous."

"Sure," I smiled. She lived in a high rise a few blocks away. We walked in silence, and she punched in the code for the door. I said goodbye, but she asked me to please have one more drink with her. I couldn't say no. So the sex wasn't as remarkable as I remembered, but it wasn't bad. It wasn't bad three times that night. As usual, I never thought that maybe I should have used a condom. But the night was fun. We talked a lot, laughed a lot. Decided that in a couple weeks we would get together again, try this on again, see if it still fit. She wanted some time to think, which I was cool with. But I also knew, if I wanted to be with someone again, someone long-term, she was right here. That was not my intent when the night started. But it did appeal to me. Get away from the Jesses of the world. Get away from the track, the gambling. Turn things around. Start a new life. A new family. Be a better father.

There was something about her that always made me think that way, but it would disappear the minute I left. Love is a bullshit, overused term. It's something we think when we are kids and our hormones are raging. It's really just about sex. But I admit, Jen was a little different. It wasn't always about sex. She could make me laugh. She could talk about almost anything. And yeah, she could fuck. Maybe I would get married again. Maybe this would be the one.

Maybe not. The last time, she was on top. I was staring at her beautiful face, and she was feeling so much bliss. You could feel it. Then my eyes fell on the mole. It was huge. It bounced up and down, staring at me, a hair hanging out of it. A flaw on an otherwise perfect painting. A booger in the Mona Lisa's nose. Jen was almost perfect. Just that damned mole. When I woke up the next morning, I kissed her on the cheek, and admired her perfect brown ass as she lay naked on the bed. "Gotta run," I whispered. "Can't wait to see you again."

She smiled. "I am so glad we did this," she whispered. "Can't wait to see you again, either." I did mean it when I said it. But it turns out I would never see her again. I wandered to my car, and had time to get home, have a quick shower, and hit the Finish Line. It was Derby Day.

BOOK 12: THE GOSPEL ACCORDING TO LOUIS CHAPTER EIGHT

I was the first one at the bar on Derby Day. Dave had opened at 10:00, and I walked in at 10:01, in hopes of maybe playing some of the early races. I really did not want to be around everyone else. I had thoughts of going to the track and playing on my own. But in the back of my mind, I knew Jesse would have something big.

I had a mint julep. It's a terrible drink, but it is the official drink of the Derby. I would probably have 10-15 before the day was over, and be sick as a dog at the end of the night. Like I said, it was a terrible drink. Jen texted me. "Did that really happen? Did I dream it?" I texted back. "Oh, it happened. And it's going to happen again. Soon." I got back a smiley face, and did not respond, because it was gambling time, and no one got in between me and Derby Day. No woman, anyway. Tickets came in in next, followed by Jesse, who was already writing things down. I saw that look and asked immediately. "What do you have, Jess?" He could not wait to tell me. "I have the ultimate Derby bomb," He was beaming. I had never seen him like this. It was like he had found the smallest needle in a mile-long hayfield. I was admittedly curious, because I had been through the field many times. I could not get past the favorite. But I could tell he was excited and could not wait to show what he had found.

"What if I were to tell you I could get you a horse with a massive jockey switch, a horse that had shown talent as a two-year-old, has been badly ridden in his last couple when they sent him to the lead -- he really wants to come from behind? And he has the perfect jockey for it?" I was puzzled. "Mine that Bird? Really?" He smiled. "Look at him. Nice horse as a two year old. The kid riding him in New Mexico was an idiot. As big a jockey switch as you will ever see. Calvin is on him, sloppy track, come from behind...and I bet we get at least 40-1."

"In Calvin we trust," I whispered. "In Calvin we trust," he said. Calvin Borel was a rider we loved. He was known for skimming the rail, and was particularly dangerous on come from behind horses. When he was riding with confidence, there was no one better. I had been riding the Borel train since his days in Louisiana and Arkansas, where he always got the best out of long shots. I was completely in love with this pick. I had to admit, it was perfect. Win or lose. Even before Jesse, we had two riders we believed in. Calvin in Kentucky and the Midwest and Victor Espinoza in California. Those two had been gold for us for years. I had a feeling Calvin was about to take us platinum. Jesse pulled $10,000 out to be our pool money. "I think we should stay away from the pick 6. I think we can spread it around with the trifecta, exactas and superfectas. Maybe the pick 3s and pick 4s. But mostly the in-race exotics. With this price we should clean up. And I think Pioneer of the Nile has to be second..."

"Agreed," I said. "And if we have the first two..." I was still pissed at Jesse, but he always had a way of making me feel like a part of it. Those were his bets, but he included me. Like it was my idea.

And I fell for it. Just like Jen had last night. Neither one of us were complaining. He smiled and started scratching down wagers. He handed the money and handwritten plays to Tickets, who was escorted out by two of Michael's men. Those guys looked damned scary. The others were trickling in, and grabbing mint juleps. By 11:00, everyone was there. We had made some other bets on the undercard, and we hit those. But the Derby...if Jesse was right... Still, I was torn. I was excited about the day, but I was also ready to turn the page. The Jen thing had muddied the waters a little. I really was thinking about giving all this up and trying it with her. So I walked over to Jesse. "Hey man," I said. "I am going to go watch at the track. I'll meet you guys to collect tomorrow, then I am outta here." He smiled at me, trying to disarm me. It wasn't working. "What's the problem, pal?"

"Jesse, this is enough. The Paks were followed home again. Pete was followed. It's time we all got out. I have had enough myself. It's not even about the disease anymore. I just want to start a new life. Get out of town."

"We are," he said. "We are heading to New Orleans. It will be fun." I was angry. "Not me, Jess. This has gone as far as I can take it. No more." He smiled and put his hand on my arm. "Let's talk tomorrow, OK? I need you there. It's important. Just promise me you won't decide until tomorrow. These people need you, too." He glanced at Sophie as he said it. "No," I said. "They don't." In the Jen afterglow, I had completely forgotten about Sophie. "You're wrong," Jesse said. "Just promise me we talk tomorrow, OK? You owe me that much." I hated him for being right, as usual. I did owe him. The bastard. Before I could answer, James busted in the door, with a gun pointed at Tickets. About 20 men piled in

135

after him, all armed. This was the nightmare that had been stalking us for weeks.

James waved his gun. "Kid won't give us the tickets, Jesse. Make him do it. No one wants this." Michael reached into his belt. His two guys were outside, guns trained on James and his gang. As badass as they were, they could not protect the kid from 20 men. They had backed off and kept their weapons, keeping a close watch. Michael got a text. I was standing behind him and saw it. "Stall them. Calvary there in 10." He whispered something to Jesse, who just nodded. James motioned for Michael to get away. "Don't make me hurt this kid." Michael's death stare was frightening. It was cold. It was dangerous. I was worried he was going to pull his weapon and kill James right there. But his voice was calm. "You aren't going to hurt this kid. In fact, you are going to let him go right now. You got a beef, you take it up with me. And my friends outside."

James looked nervous. Jesse walked over to him, looking deep in his eyes. "James, let the kid go. You don't want to do this. See his friends outside? He has about 20 more coming. Put the gun down and I make sure they leave you alone. Do we really want to spend Derby Day in a gunfight?"

"Fuck that," Michael said. "He was a dead man the second he put that gun at my cousin's head. You hear me trucker? You and your fucking pals are already dead." Jesse snapped. "Shut up, Mike.

Nobody is going to kill anybody today. Everybody lower your weapons, and we will settle this." What happened next shocked me. All of James' people lowered their weapons, and let Tickets go. Maybe I learned something that day. They really weren't bad people. They were just desperate. We had all been desperate once. I think I understood then. In fact, they at least had the balls to try something. If Jesse had not fallen in my lap, I could not have done that. And what they had been asking for was not unreasonable at all.

Michael's guys, however, did not lower their guns. I saw the text on Michael's phone. "Clean it up?" Jesse looked at Michael, and Tickets ran over and stood next to him. He seemed completely unaffected. "Sorry boss," the kid said. "Caught me by surprise. I got the tickets. Wouldn't give them up for anything." Michael smiled at the kid and patted him on the back, like a proud father. Jesse just shook his head at Michael, who texted back "stand down. See if we can do this peaceful." The men lowered their weapons, but did not put them down. I could tell they had been in bad situations. I suspected they could "clean" the whole thing up in a matter of seconds now that there weren't 20 guns trained on the kid. Jesse raised his arms and stood on the bar. "So this...this is what we've come to? We threaten a kid? We are willing to die just to steal someone else's tickets? Is money that important to all of you?" Most of them nodded yes.

"Think about this. If you stole those tickets, you would not live the day. If you shot that kid, you would be in jail. Or worse. There's no escape here. You see those two outside? They could kill everyone in the room. What would you have then? What would your family have? "Nothing. So you were all willing to die today, basically. And none of you are bad men." Everyone was mesmerized. I was disgusted. The con man was at it again. "So you fucked up. We all have, man. We've cheated on our wives. We've screwed friends out of jobs. We've talked girls into abortions and could never let go of it." At this, James' face turned dark. Jesse struck a nerve.

"And none of us -- none of us are bad people." He paused to take a drink. The room was silent. Even Michael's men were locked in. "You know what you are all forgetting????" His voice turned to a whisper. This is all we have, guys. We are supposed to enjoy it. We are supposed to live our life every day like it's our last. There is nothing guaranteed. Religion? A joke created to keep people in line. And that's scary for us, because without some kind of moral code, what are we? But with that code, are we better? Do we punish ourselves for a lifetime for one mistake?" He looked at one of Michael's men.

"Do you punish yourself every night for what you were ordered to do in Iraq? Do you do what you do now because you are beyond redemption?" He looked at James. "Going along with an abortion is hard. You grew up Catholic. That guilt is supposed to be with you. But it's all a lie. "It's all a giant fucking lie. Look at all of you. You are beating yourselves up over things from your past that just happen. We don't have to be proud of them. We just have to refuse to let them define us."

He paused and had another drink. By now, he had them all. He knew it. Just like I knew it the night before. "So how do we define ourselves?

138

By what makes us happy. For too many of you, it's money." He waved his arm towards us, and I thought he was pointing directly at me. "Do they look happy? And they have more money than they will ever need. Money is no god, either." They were confused. Jesse had them twisted. "Do you want to know? Do you really want to know why you are here?" Everyone nodded except me. I was long out on this B.S. I suspected Jesse was just stalling for the cavalry.

"Are you familiar with Plato's Parable of the Cave?" Almost none of them were. I was. It was his go-to every time we were high. Hoo boy. Here we go. "Imagine a group of people tied up, with a fire behind them. The only thing they see are shadows on the walls. That's their life. The shadows could be anything. Your life. Those tickets you wanted. That is all you see. But then someone comes and takes them outside the cave, and they see the entire world. And they realize what they thought was their reality was nothing but shadows on a wall. And that's the way you have been living your lives. Guilt. Greed. Failure. Just shadows on a wall, man. Shadows on a fucking wall…But you don't have to stay there. Come with me outside the cave. Give up those shadows. Not everyone can. Not everyone wants to. But if you want to understand life, if you want true enlightenment…if you want to realize we are all part of the same, common consciousness, that spirituality isn't confession, it isn't some concept of heaven or hell…It's us. Walking outside the cave. Seeing the world with wonder.

Finding what truly makes us happy.

"Yes, I can give you a winner today. And I will. But money won't solve your problems. Money is just a way for bored people to keep score. If you want true greatness, true enlightenment, find your world outside the cave. A lot of it will be like mine. But most of it will be yours. You came in here with guns today. And you are going to leave with a winner and a message. Which do you think is more important?" They all just stared. completely mesmerized. "You know what makes me happiest?" Jesse asked.

"Fucking my girlfriend in a threesome?" I thought. Sorry, couldn't resist. The others nodded, completely hooked. "Making these people money. And slowly watching them realize that it is not important." He smiled at me. "Louis gets it. He just wants to get back to being a weed-smoking, track degenerate writer. Tell stories. That's his world. And it's a good one. And when he stops beating himself up for mistakes past and mistakes to come, he will get there." Jesse was wrong. Past mistakes? They never bothered me. The mistakes to come had me a little worried, though. By now, four black SUVs had pulled up. The cavalry was there. Michael fired off a quick text. "Now I am going to give you that horse today. All of you. I am not going to tell you how to bet it, or give you money. How you play it is up to you. But I am not doing this because you threatened us. Or because I think you will be happy when you win. I'm doing it because in order to get out of the cave, someone has to lead you. And this is how I am going to do it. But I want a promise from every one of you...."

Again, everyone was nodding feverishly. Men were out of the trucks, also equally mesmerized. "When you get outside that cave...when you find enlightenment...show others the way. Bring them where I am bringing you. And you know what? All that crap you've let define you? It will wash away. You just have to let it." James was in tears, and so were most of his men. "I'm sorry. I really am. I didn't understand..." Jesse smiled. "Don't you see? Don't be sorry. Just leave the cave. Come join the world with us."

Mare reached her arms around Jesse and hugged him from behind. The others all pressed forward, wanting to shake his hand. To touch him. It was all too much for me. I started to leave. Michael stopped me. It was clear he was moved. "Where you going kid?"

I softened a little. "Going to go watch at the track. I think the con man has made it safe for us now." Michael laughed at me. "We will talk tomorrow." He had sounded just like Jesse.

As I left, I heard Jesse tell them all: "I gave James the horse. He will give it to you. Don't blow this. There won't be another one. Make sure you at least put some win money on it. Don't let greed keep you in the cave." I walked out, right past Michael's guys, who were chatting amongst themselves. The weapons had been put away. Even the mob henchmen were moved. But they quickly got in the SUV and left. I suspected Franie V. himself might have been in one of those cars, and I don't think he wanted Michael to see he had come to handle this if necessary. After reading some of Michael's work, I am sure it was him. And it would have made sense that no one would see him, because I believe he wanted out of that life. And he would have only dove in that hard for Michael. Just like Michael had for him. If it was Frankie V., he had the horse, too. Michael would have told him. I wasn't surprised the SUV headed straight to the race track.

Jesse had moved them all. Maybe even Frankie V. Not me. Fuck it. Con man. This was all over the top. And with each moment I was realizing that getting completely out was the right move. Hell, maybe just leave the track tonight, surprise Jen at her place and never leave. Never see any of these people again. Well, maybe after the trial. Screw it. It was time to bet.

I got to the track, and it was packed to the hilt. I finally gave up on the mint juleps and went back to Jack. I knew all our tickets were in, but I decided to do something on my own. Play the superfecta. I remembered my conversation with Jesse that morning. We had the first two horses, so I could just put everybody in third and fourth, and I would be good. So I went to a teller I knew well, one that I actually trusted. We had learned who was talking, and I was avoiding them at all costs. I bet an 8 with 16 with all with all superfecta for $1. It was a $272 ticket. The teller thought I was crazy. I just laughed and said "what the hell? Gotta take a swing every now and then."

I wandered around and took in the sights. Beautiful girls dressed to the nines. Most of them in lavish hats. Man, there was something about a woman in a hat. Jen looked great in hats. I shook her out of my mind, wandered around enjoying the scenery and trying to scout out which of these ladies was without male companionship. The track levels were kind of like society itself. The suite level was where the hyper rich hung out; oil tycoons, sports team owners, the richest of the rich. The quality of women reflected it. But the average human being could not get anywhere near the suite level on Derby Day. Security would not let them.

The second level was upper crust that wasn't filthy rich. Doctors. Lawyers. Oil and gas. And the quality of women was outstanding. I was hanging out on this floor most of the day, mainly because I knew the semi-hidden teller where I would not have to wait in line for bets. On Derby Day, you always waited in line. But after my bets were in, I decided to try something different.

The first floor was for people who could barely afford to be there. Dirty clothes, cheap beer, ragged women. For some reason, I decided to go down here to watch the race, outside on the track apron, where they would show it on the big screen. There was live racing going on as well, but it was quarter horses, so nobody really cared. It was down here that I saw James. I didn't want to talk to him, but he approached me anyway. "Hey, Louis, I can't tell you how sorry I am. Win or lose, I learned a lot today." I felt a little sorry for him, like I did when he first put down his weapon. I smiled. "No need to apologize," I said. "It's done with. So how did you play the race?"

"Well, I only have $200 to my name. So I put $100 to win, then played the trifecta a bunch of times with him on top, Pioneer in second and everybody in third." Maybe I just had been caught up in Jesse's BS, but I really was feeling sorry for James. And man, Jen kept popping in my head, telling me I had changed. Maybe I wanted her to be right. "Hey, look, if you want to borrow another few hundred…"

He smiled. "No thanks, Louis. But damned, this day is full of surprises. You are the last guy I would ever think would want to help me." I laughed. "Tell you what...here's another $200. Make the same bets again and we will split them. Can pay me back when it hits." He nodded and took two crisp Benjamins. "You sure, Louis? I had a gun on you guys just a couple hours ago." I laughed. "Of course I'm sure. Did you learn nothing from Jesse's speech?" He nodded knowingly. Yes, he had learned something. I gave him a playful punch on the shoulder. "Let me buy your drinks, since you spent all your money betting."

That he also agreed to, and we went to find a quiet spot to watch the races. But at a Derby Day at the track, there was no quiet spot. We settled on going back outside, in front of the big screen on the tote board. It was damned hot that day, which is why most people were staying in the air conditioned comfort. It did not bother us, because our drinks were cold. We made small talk, joked around a bit. James finally asked. "Jesse…is he...Jesus? I know it sounds stupid…" The anger welled up. But James had undergone some kind of transformation. I didn't want to destroy that. I wanted to do the right thing. I wanted to show Jen I had really changed. "Honestly? I doubt it. But yeah, James, there is something special about him." I felt pretty good about that response. James seemed to like it, too. We toasted and waited for the horses to enter the gate for the Kentucky Derby. "What a weird fucking day," I said to no one in particular. When Mine That Bird, a 50-1 long shot, crossed the wire first by a large margin, the entire place went dead silent. The only noise was one of James' friends screaming at the top of his lungs from the other end of the grandstand. James smiled, but hardly said anything. He just started crying. I put my arm on his shoulder, "Feels good, huh?"

"No," he said. "It feels weird. Jesse was right. I did not need this." James made $5,000 on his win bet. He had the trifecta 5 times for $100,000. The two of us split the same bet for half that each. My superfecta paid over $225,000. My group had it five more times. We also had the trifecta 10 times, the pick 4 for $10,000 ten times, and the pick three 20 times for $2,905. And several thousand dollars in win, place and show bets. It would be our largest score. And yet like James had said, it felt weird. The disease really wasn't about needing to win. The disease was about the rush. Betting enough to make it hurt if you lose. So when you win, it is all that much sweeter. But only winning? It was hard to appreciate. Because there was no hurt. No loss. No risk. This wasn't gambling anymore. And while it had made me rich, it wasn't fun anymore, either. It had taken me this long to figure it out. James got it right away. Jen was right. I had changed.

I decided to wander back to the Finish Line after I cashed my ticket. The place was packed with all of Jesse's new friends. Jesse came straight over to me. "Well? Feeling good Louis?" I laughed and thought of *Trading Places*. "No man." I was really drunk by now, as usual. I couldn't enjoy the moment. I had to ask. I was in a weird place, and I wanted to know. "Who the fuck are you man?" He smiled. "A man. Just like you." I sneered. "Whatever, man. Can we stop now? We damned

sure don't need the money. And I am not even enjoying it anymore."
Pete, of all people, came over. "We can't stop, Louis. You know that. It's
what we are. This is our world outside the cave." I finally skulked off to
my seat at the bar, knowing I wasn't winning anyone over today, when
Sophie finally cornered me. We had not talked in weeks. I did not want
to talk then. "Louis, I know you have been avoiding me…"

"It's nothing personal, honey, I've just been bus.." She interrupted.
"Louis, I'm pregnant. I'm going to have it. Come to New Orleans with
us and we will talk it out."

It felt strange. "It's mine?" I asked. Somewhere deep down, I had
already known what this was about. It was something I had suspected but
never really thought about. I also had the same, weird feeling about Jen
last night. We never discussed birth control. Fucking stupid. "99 percent
sure, yeah," she said. Again, jealousy flashed over me. "99 percent? So
there is a one percent chance it isn't? Whose then?" I already knew. She
knew I did. She didn't have to say the name. "He didn't cum in me," she
said. "Just Mare. But we were all so drunk. Still, the timing doesn't work.
It's yours. We need to talk this out, Louis. I'm sorry. It all just happened.
After you I felt free again. I was alive again for the first time in years. I
still am. Please...let's work it out, OK?"

I glared at her, then Jesse. "Fuck this, man." Sophie grabbed my arm,
her eyes begging me to stay. I just snapped away and kept going. I lit up
a joint as soon as I got outside. My mind was drunk and racing. Another
kid? I already paid a shitload of child support for three I never saw. And
this one might be fucking Jesse's. Just when the thing with Jen lights

back up, I have this to deal with. Fuck. What now? I was way too messed up to think. Drunk. High. Emotional. I decided I would go back tomorrow and say my goodbyes. And figure out what to do about Sophie. But then I passed out in the bushes in the parking lot. Apparently no one noticed. I woke up the next morning, smelling of piss and Jack Daniels.

BOOK 13: THE GOSPEL ACCORDING TO MARE CHAPTER ONE

My name is Mare. If Louis has done this right, you know a lot about me already. Jesse asked me to write a journal and give it to Louis. Hopefully he makes me sound intelligent. I am not a writer. I'm a former stripper, a former prostitute. A woman who fucked up her daughter's life. But I am none of those things anymore. That's what Jesse taught us. That's what I hope to teach others.

We were worried about Louis. I don't know if it was the thing with Sophie, the alcohol, the concerns about all the people showing up...But he was drifting away from us. And we needed Louis. I had always liked him. He liked to think he was smarter than everybody else, and he probably was. Like all of us, he drank too damned much. He was emotional. He would go from loving you to hating you in a day. He was a terrific writer, and I supposed he needed the emotion for that. I think Sophie described him best. She said he was "messy."

I think that was a fair term. He would show up at the club all the time. He took girls in the back every time, but he seemed to think it would be awkward with me. Hell, it was just business. Wouldn't have meant a damned thing. But that's not how Louis' mind worked. Honestly, I wouldn't be surprised if he was a little undiagnosed bi- polar. Not enough to be violent, but enough that you never knew if he was going to tell you he loved you or bite your head off over something stupid. For all his experience, Louis was still an emotional teen-ager. But at his best, he could be brilliant and funny. We were seeing that less and less. When he drank a little, he was good Louis. A lot? He was moody, childish and a little mean. We loved him anyway. Especially good Louis. I came to the track one day after a particularly rough night with a very, let's say, physically aggressive client. I was feeling worthless. Louis was the only one there and it was a good Louis day. "You look like you could use some cheering up," he said. I managed a fake smile. "You have no idea."

He was cleaned up this day, and was actually an attractive man. If not for the spotty personality, he would be a hell of a catch. But you just knew you would wake up one morning and wonder what the hell you had gotten yourself into. Louis wasn't violent. But the constant tennis match that was his emotional state would drive even the most normal woman insane. And how many of us are really normal?

He laughed. "I heard a joke…" I was surprised. Louis didn't tell jokes. He was funny, but it was always an improv, in the moment, riffing off someone else's thing. "Ok...shoot," I said. "How do you get a witch pregnant?" I smiled. "I honestly have no idea." He deadpanned, "you fuck her." OK, it was truly awful. But it made my day. He could do that, more often than not. And when he was petulant Louis, he just kept to himself. For the longest time his personality was easy to read based on winning and losing. But after we all starting winning, it went the other way. I think deep down Louis needed his misery to enjoy the good times.

Misery was his emotional base. Misery was his muse. Without it, he had no frame of reference for happiness. It was kind of sad, really. I don't think he meant to, but Jesse's success took away Louis' soul. That's why I could never blame him for anything. None of us ever did. Louis was a tragedy. So brilliant. So tortured. But you know what? In my business I met a lot of brilliant people. Men and women both. The more creative and smart they were, the more demons they had. I just thought they let the demons bother them too much. But I imagine if you were smart enough to know the things those people know, you could never truly be happy. Those of us who didn't think about things all the time...well, maybe it was easier. I'll never get over Lilly, that's true. But that's obvious. These people worried about the strangest things, Louis most of all. Like not wanting to sleep with me for business. Who cares? Or getting pissed at Sophie for doing a threesome with us. It was just drunk fun. It wasn't worth brooding over.

The Sunday after the Derby, Jesse and I went to Louis' place. He wasn't there. We waited an hour or so before he finally staggered up, wearing last night's clothes, having pissed all over himself. He was not happy to see us. "What the fuck do you two want?" He sneered. He was clearly still drunk. "We brought your cut," Jesse said. "And I just want to talk." Louis opened the door to his apartment, not really inviting us in but not objecting, either. "I need a shower. Give me a minute." That was Louis. Pissed at Jesse, but not enough to tell us to leave. The apartment wasn't much. A couch, a TV, a desk with a laptop. No art, nothing. It was plain, the kind of place you stayed in but did not live in. The only thing that stood out was a picture of three kids on the desk. Louis never talked about them. When Louis emerged, he looked like a new man. It was amazing how a shower could wash away a hangover in a hurry. We all had that skill.

Jesse tossed him the bag. "There ya go, amigo. Mine that Bird," Louis was relaxing a little. "Mine that Bird..." his voice trailed off. Jesse turned stern. "Come meet us at the bar later. Let's make plans for New Orleans. I know you are pissed at me, and I am sorry for that. But we have some important business there. Then I promise you can go your own way if you want." Louis stared, silent for a long time. "I'm being a dick again, aren't I?" I smiled. "Little bit..." He laughed. "Sorry guys. Been drinking too much. Did I do anything stupid last night?" Jesse laughed. "No, man. But you might want to apologize to Sophie."

"Fuck me.." He was clearly starting to remember. "Sophie..." His mind started putting stuff together. His eyes flashed dark, but then good Louis returned. "You guys want to watch a movie before we go? I've got *I, Robot*..." It seemed like a strange suggestion, but Jesse loved the idea. We got high, watched I Robot, and then all went to the bar together, Jesse and Louis the entire walk debating the deeper meaning of humanity in the movie and how it all somehow applied to the Patriot Act. In a Will Smith movie. Right, guys. One big happy family, for now. Louis had apparently learned another joke. He told it as we were approaching the bar. "So," he says. "Superman is flying around one day. He sees Wonder Woman lying in her back yard naked, taking in some sun. He had always wanted to hit that, but she never seemed all that interested. So he thinks about it. 'Hey, I'm Superman. I can zip down there, hit it fast, and she'll never know. I will be 20 miles away before she even notices.'

So he does. Bam. Gone. Wonder Woman, shocked, says 'what the hell was that?'

The Invisible Man says 'I don't know, but it hurt like hell.'" I wish this Louis was around more often. He was frantically texting somebody, too, and smiled every time he got a text back. I did not know what that was about. But I was pretty sure it wasn't Sophie. The Finish Line was packed. More people than ever were there to see Jesse. And none of them wanted winners. They just wanted to see the man. See if he was truly special. See if he was who they thought he was. I guess you know by now what I believe. Never had a doubt. Everyone wanted another speech from Jesse. He smiled, took a few minutes to talk to everyone, encourage them. He looked over at me. "You guys should listen to Mare."

The place went silent. It's funny, I was always the center of attention, but this was different. They were watching me in a different way. It wasn't an "I want to fuck you" look. They wanted to hear what I had to say. It was an amazing feeling. Nobody had ever cared about what I said before; just what I could do for them and how much it would cost.

"Happy Sunday," I said. They responded in kind. "We all feel a little different today, don't we?" I asked. They all nodded, especially James, who was hanging on every word. "I have felt that way since Jesse came into my life. So have my friends. And it's important we make others feel that way." The words were coming out as if someone else were saying them. It was all so natural. It was as if Jesse were speaking through me. Or maybe even Louis. A lot of you know what I did for a living. I did business with many of you. Some called me a whore. But is that what I was? Is that how I defined myself? The truth is, I didn't care how you defined me. It was a job. I make no apologies. If I had to go back, I would. But I don't have to go back. Some of you might know what happened to my daughter. It was terrible. I have had to live with that. I punished myself. I wanted to die.

"I thought the more bad things I did to myself, the more I deserved it. That's why I think I was relieved when the doctors told me they thought I had cancer. It was fair penance. But what happened to my daughter -- it wasn't my fault. It was the fault of a sick man. It was a tragedy." Their eyes were all on me, all lit up. Hanging on every word. "I can't change it. But I don't have to let it destroy both our lives. Jesse taught me that." I paused. I was enjoying this. And it was easy, because it was all true. "Jesse told me the doctors were wrong about my cancer. Turns out they were. I do not have breast cancer. But I also believe when Jesse touched me, he took that cancer away. He says that's not the case. Does it matter? Either way, no cancer. And I'm glad. I want to live. And I deserve to be a mother again. They did tell me I was pregnant. With a little girl. I'm getting a second chance. I deserve that, too."

I took in the ooohs and aahhs of the crowd. "But we don't need second chances. We just need to realize we are going to make mistakes. Some of them are bad. But they can't define us. If we accept that, then it's not about second chances. It's about what we do each day. The beauty in life is out there every single day, even if we happen to overlook it. It's time to stop ignoring it." They applauded. It was loud. Raucous. Michael came over to me, a look of concern. "Great speech...but please talk to Jesse.

We need to get the hell out of here. This is too big for us." I was mildly irritated. This was my moment, and all Michael could think about was getting out. "Look what we are doing," I said. "This is important."

He gave me that stern, dad-like look. "Just talk to Jesse, OK, honey? We don't need this." Deep down, I agreed we needed to do something. We would never be able to just be a group again, not like before. But I did not want to let go of this rush. I wanted it every day. This was better than winning. This was changing lives. This was truly being important. How many people get to feel that way? Jesse had already figured out what Michael wanted, and came over to me. He did look concerned. "Let's meet tomorrow," Jesse said. "Get everybody together at Sophie's place? Noon? We should all talk. Michael's right." Jesse started pulling aside people and talking to them one on one. Some of them just wanted to touch him. Some wanted to hear him. Even Jesse seemed a little uncomfortable with it all. Now they were approaching me the same way, as if I were Jesse. And I loved every minute of it.

It went on for a couple hours, and then people started to file out. When it was down to just a few of us, I noticed Jesse was deep in conversation with James, who was eating it up. Louis and Sophie were talking cordially. I had not realized how many people were there when I was talking. Now that I saw it clear out, I knew Michael was right. Even the Finish Line would never be private for us again. But I felt part of something bigger. Maybe it was supposed to be this way. And maybe I was supposed to be the one they came to see. Maybe – just maybe – this was only the beginning of something huge. I knew at that moment what my future would be about. What my world outside the cave would become.

That night, Jesse and I were in bed, and he seemed a little sad. He had been procrastinating on the New Orleans trip, but he realized we could not do that anymore. "OK, we tell everyone tomorrow. Let's rent one of those fancy limo busses. James can drive." I objected. I thought we could do so many more things right here in Houston. But Jesse had other ideas. He sighed deeply. "We have big things to do there, Mare. I want you to write things down, OK? Like today. I want you to tell that story, and give it to Louis. It's going to be important." I did not like his tone. "Is everything going to be OK? And are you sure we need to leave? We are building something here. We can do a lot more. I can do a lot more…" And I wanted to do so much more. I wanted that rush every day. I wanted people hanging on every word. Not even noticing my tits.

He smiled. "Of course, it's going to be OK. You took a big step today, Mare. People will follow you. Lead them to the right place. And your time is coming. But we have business elsewhere first. We have one more step we have to take. After that, it's going to build on its own. And you are going to be a big part of it all." I did not know what he meant, but I had learned to trust in him completely. I had faith in Jesse Christian. I knew him. I knew who he really was. And I would have followed him anywhere. Even to New Orleans.

BOOK 14: THE GOSPEL ACCORDING TO MARE CHAPTER TWO

The "bus" was one of the most lavish things I had ever seen. It looked like what I imagined the inside of a private jet would be. The bathroom took up four rows. The bar took up four more. There was a private room in the back, where you could take a "nap." I'm guessing it wasn't used for that very often. Jesse and I did not nap in it. I'm guessing Louis and Sophie didn't, either. They seemed to be getting along fine again, which is what we needed. Louis had a big role to play, and we knew how flighty he could be. He had this Dallas thing in his head, and it never took much to set him off. Sophie was keeping him calm.

I had rented the bus, but we had to pay extra, because they wanted their own driver. Jesse had wanted James, for a lot of reasons. We were going to talk on the way over, and these stories were not going to be for strangers. We had crossed the border on I-10, going over the Sabine River bridge into Louisiana, passing Vinton, the home of Delta Downs, another racetrack we had frequented on occasion. In the old days, we would have stopped for the day, but no one was interested. No one even mentioned it. Then again, there was always Evangeline Downs just more than an hour away. And Fair Grounds in New Orleans. There was always another racetrack.

Louisiana was flat, tree-lined. The trip to New Orleans included crossing the Mississippi River, and a long stretch over a swamp. It wasn't a pretty drive, but I have seen a lot worse. The thing that stood out was all the little casinos. They were basically glorified gas stations with slot machines and cheesy names like Casino Aces and Slot Magic. There were at least two at every exit. At my lowest point, I could never have imagined going into those places. The desperation it must have taken made our lives before Jesse look positively glorious. Jesse was tending bar, dealing out drinks. He had cranked out some pretty potent margaritas in the vehicle's margarita machine. Everybody loved them. The sharp bite of the tequila, the cold head rush that came from drinking the frozen concoction too fast. We were all feeling it. All except James, who refused to drink while driving the bus. He was surprising me more and more every day. He seemed to understand Jesse better than any of us, maybe even me. Jesse banged glasses together, trying to get everyone's attention. "So if I can have a minute, I want to thank all of you for coming." They laughed. None of them except Louis would have missed it for the world.

"So I have rooms booked for us at the Hilton. We are paid up for two weeks. Everyone enjoy themselves. You are pretty much on your own. I just ask that you all meet me for supper on Thursday night. I have reserved a private room at an Italian restaurant in the Quarter. Mare will text you the info. It's my treat. Will you do that for me?" Everyone nodded. He raised his glass. "I want to toast all of you. To good friends, winning tickets, and changing how we view the world."

Everyone enthusiastically drank to that. Louis kind of half-assed it, but he always did that. "Mare told her story the other day. It moved a lot of you. She had as much to let go of as anyone. So we have some time. Does anybody else want to let something go? Show that you've moved on? Alan was the first, telling the Big Jim story. Jesse hugged him when it was over. "That was never your guilt, you know," he said. Alan nodded. "But somebody had to take responsibility." While his words trailed off, Big Jim surprised us, telling his end of it. "Spider is the only one who knows this, but ah knew those boys were trying to fix that game. Hell, they were my roommates. ah should have gone straight to coach. But ah didn't want to get those guys in trouble. If ah had done the right thing, Spider would have never had to feel guilty."

"And how do you feel about it now?" Jesse asked. Big Jim smiled. He really was just a goofy kid. "Like ah do 'bout everything, Jess. Can't change yesterday. But I damned sure am fixin' to shape tomorrow." Smiles were everywhere. Except Louis, of course. I wasn't sure why Jesse called him out. "What about you, Louis?" He was clearly irritated, but he was trying hard to fit in and keep things smooth with Jesse. "What do you want me to say? I'm a shit writer? A bad father? Terrible husband? Drink too much? Gamble too much? Womanize too much? Let the dumbest things bother me? Guilty on all counts. But I never had any great sin to get over. I didn't need redemption. I was always those things. And I always will be. So I don't need the great catharsis. I take myself for what I am."

Jesse seemed satisfied with that. "Louis always got it," he said.

"That's why he is here. But this isn't about your "sin." What is sin anyway? What the Bible tells us? A book written by people we don't

158

know about other people who might not have even existed? A wise man once told me sin is like shooting an arrow at a target. Sometimes we miss. So the next time we just adjust." Jesse was always so great when he got going. "So don't do this or you go to hell? What is hell? What could be worse for Mare than losing her child? That's hell. But there's some torture chamber when you die? That's it? Some grand battle for the souls of men? Doesn't that seem silly?

"If you look at what Jesus really said, was it much different than Plato? Try to be enlightened? Achieve gnosis? Maybe his words were slapped together, combined with a vengeful, tribal god to scare everyone into submission so the Catholic church would run everything. And all the while his true message was ignored. Because he wasn't about power or control. Now that doesn't mean there's NOT a hell. Or a heaven. But imagine if hell were what we dealt with on earth. What everyone deals with every day. And heaven is really just an understanding that we are all part of the same holistic collective, that we all have something in common? That when we hurt others we really hurt ourselves? Wouldn't that make for a better world?"

Other than with me, Jesse had rarely shared his thoughts until the last few days. And we ate up every word. "Jesus made so many great points. But then his words were twisted, translated, re-worked to fit the power structure. We should use those teachings. But they are just that, teachings. You know why religion is so popular? So it can think for us. Imagine what the world would be like if our moral vision of right and wrong came from ourselves? No one wants that responsibility. But once you take it, once you embrace it...the world is a better place. You don't hide as a priest and rape kids. You don't fly planes into buildings in the name of being a martyr. You don't collect millions from lonely old people by playing on their emotions. "You just do the right thing as often as you can. And when you miss the target, you take another shot. John Lennon saw it. Why can't we all?" His words hung in the air. I think I loved him more at that moment than ever. "Who is next?"

Pete, quiet Pete, stepped up. "I was in a car crash a few years ago. My wife was killed. Nice young lady, good family. We had been out to dinner. It was raining -- one of those typical Texas summer storms, where you can barely see. Well, a damned dog runs right in front of us. I try to avoid it, and we crash into a concrete ditch. I thought I was a goner for sure. When I woke up, Jeannie was choking on her seat belt. I tried to break free, and then I just stopped and watched. I wasn't sure I could have done anything anyway; I had a pretty bad concussion. But I did not even try. It only took about 15 seconds, but it seemed like forever before she died. The look in her eyes. The betrayal. I felt terrible immediately. But I also felt relief. She never did anything wrong. She didn't deserve to die like that.

"The paramedics said her sternum was crushed and she was going to bleed to death anyway, and that it was probably a lot less painless the way she went. But that damned sure wasn't my intent. I'm gay. I never wanted to be married to a woman. I just saw it as a way out. So I watched her die. Wasn't her fault I'm gay. None of it was her fault. And she is the one who died. It wasn't until Jesse's speech the other day that I forgave myself for that. I can finally be myself. " Jesse gave him one of those hugs. Pete kissed him on the cheek. Everyone toasted. "To Gay Pete!" Big Jim drawled. Pete laughed. We all did.

Sophie was next. Everyone agreed hers really wasn't that bad. "I agree," she said. "We have all fucked up, guys. But here we are. It's not what we've done, it's what we do next." She looked right at Louis when she said it. Then came Bernie the Dentist. His was simply hating being a dentist, and everything about it. He told the story of the Fruity Pebbles again, and everyone reminded him we already heard it. But he said he could never be around that cereal again. One of his kids had been eating it one morning at breakfast and Bernie threw up. He cheated on his taxes. He lied to his wife. He felt bad about not wanting to be a dentist. Nothing like the others, but then we all did not have horrible pasts. We were just unhappy for different reasons. Bernie's guilt came from doing a job he hated to make his parents happy, then basically leaving his wife to do all the work while he stayed at the track all the time. Poor Bernie. His guilt just wasn't as interesting as everyone else's. What the hell. He was a dentist.

Big Paul admitted he screwed his old law partner over, forcing him out so Little Paul could move in. The man had deteriorated fast after that. The job was all that was holding him together. He OD'd on heroin and died a year later. Both Pauls struggled with that. Big Paul admitted the man was on that path anyway, which is one of the reasons why he wanted him out. Still, it stayed with them. Then there were The Paks. I felt terrible for calling them that. Belal and Sonia were their names, not that anybody knew. Belal told the story of the man Sonia was supposed to marry. Like them, he was from an extremely rich family, and the marriage was arranged. But Belal and Sonia had become close, and their families were OK with that match, too. The man wasn't. The other man, sensing he was losing Sonia, broke into her home and raped her in her room, thinking that would make Belal not want her. But afterward Sonia stabbed him in the neck with a pair of scissors, hitting the carotid artery and killing him in less than a minute. Belal came to her aid immediately. They fled the country before anyone found the body. Belal knew that even as well- to do as Sonia's family was, she would not avoid trial. And the man's family would want justice. And in their culture, the man would win. It was an accident – she did not intend to kill him, merely defend herself and prevent a second rape. But a man from an important family was dead and someone had to pay. Belal would not let it happen.

Their families wired them a substantial amount of money. They bought new identities in England and came to the States on U.S. passports. It was amazing how easy it was to forge who they were. Even after 911, it just took money. It made Belal wonder how many terrorists got in the same way. But they were not terrorists. They were a murderer and her lover. They knew no one. They had no friends, no jobs, and with the money from their parents, no real need to get jobs.

Somehow they wound up at the track one day and never left. Their parents warned them to never contact them again, so they were cut off from that world. Our little group was the only family they had now.

Making it worse was the fact that the man Sonia had killed had been Belal's cousin. He had wronged her, but killing him was too much. It was never her intent, but the scissors hit the right spot. They both had to live with that. And never seeing anyone they ever cared about ever again, for the rest of their lives. When they finished their story, alternating parts of it in broken English, I saw them transform. They looked younger, like the kids who had fled Pakistan. Their faces glowed. They smiled, maybe for the first time I could remember. As they hugged everyone, it was obvious; Belal and Sonia and had found a family. They had found a home, a better one that what they fled for a single moment's anger many years ago. And here they would always be safe. And the fact that they could finally tell someone who they really were, with no fear of retribution...It changed their world forever.

Michael was last. The bus was silent, because we all knew Michael's background. "I'm not going to tell you what you want to hear," Michael said. "I am writing some things down. When I am gone, you can read about what I did. Just know I am worse than all of you. There is no salvation, and I am good with that." He smiled. "You know, how we would always just hope to get that one big score to get back to even and start all over?" Everyone nodded. Sophie smiled knowingly.

"I think a lot of people are like that. Let me do one big thing to get back to even for all the bad. Save a baby from a burning building. Risk your life to pull someone out of a burning car. Rescue people from a plane crash. Do something like that, and we are back to even as human beings. "But in my case? Add up every possibility, and it wouldn't even get me close to even.".

He then told the story of Frankie Jr., although that wasn't the name he used. There was silence when he finished. Except for Pete. "Have you tried a 4-iron? Much less loft, not much harder to hit. A lot more damage around the knees and ankles." Everyone laughed. More margaritas lost their lives. The whole gang was happy. Louis clearly wasn't, but even he managed to disappear to the private room with Sophie for a while.

We were passing through Baton Rouge, home of the LSU Tigers. One thing I liked about Louisiana? You could buy alcohol at convenience stores. In Texas it was only beer and wine. We stopped, re-loaded on tequila and Jack and I bought an LSU tank top while we were there. Purple always looked good on me. We all chatted the last leg of the drive. Pete was a lot more interesting than I had ever known. He was a geologist, and had a love of dinosaurs. He had traveled all over the world, to exotic places. Dubai. China. Australia. He had great stories from all of his travels. I wished he had come out of the closet years ago. Big Paul, Michael and Bernie had a pretty contentious poker game going. Michael was making dentist jokes, and raking most of the pots. Every time he beat Bernie out of a pot, he would yell "Fruity Pebbles, bitch!" Bernie laughed every time and started calling Michael "Tiger Woods."

It was, in my mind. all of our lives at their very best. For all the crap we had done, we had given ourselves...for all the failures...we had come out of the cave. And we were going to bring a lot more with us. A bunch of gamblers. Misfits. Whores. Our world had changed. And there was much more to come. Louis and Sophie returned, both looking relaxed. We were getting good Louis again. "You guys have been getting way too fucking spiritual lately," he said. "Let's get drunk and tell inappropriate jokes." I smiled. It was good seeing him like that. "Tell them your Superman joke..." It had officially become a party bus.

BOOK 15: THE GOSPEL ACCORDING TO LOUIS CHAPTER NINE

Ah, the Silverthorn Casino. A riverboat dump. My kind of place. It was dirty. Even the chips were disgusting. The place was filled with old people on Rascals, hooked up to oxygen, chain smoking the whole time, playing two, three slot machines at once. The poker room was wild and full of fools, the blackjack tables covered with idiots who could ruin your night with their own bad plays. Pop music played constantly over the loudspeakers.

And oh, the oxygen they pumped into the place. It was there to keep you awake, keep you gambling. And the noise...the constant ringing of bells on the slot machines. Every so often, a "wheel...of...fortune!" The occasional roar from the craps table. An Asian screaming "monkey!" Women for hire and women just trying to look good, all dressed the same. Little black dresses, big heels. I loved casinos. As much as I loved the track, a casino was better. More desperation. More degeneracy. More failure.

I had gotten a couple hours sleep after we arrived, then began my New Orleans routine. Start touristy -- Pat O'Brien's for two hurricanes, but no more than that. Anything beyond that and you were done if you drank anything else. Then down the street to the Opera House for drinks, live music and jello shots off the chests of young girls. Then, finally the casino, though by now I was pretty much gone. At each stop, I would text Jen, telling her I missed her. She would respond by telling me to get my ass to Houston. I had told her I was on a job interview. It was easy to lie to her. But I promised I would spend all my time with her when we got back. She couldn't wait. Once I hit the casino, though, the texts stopped. You know me by now.

Everyone had kind of gone their separate ways on this day. I saw Jesse and Mike playing blackjack, but made a conscience effort to not be spotted. Sophie was in the poker room and seemed to be doing well. I got on the list for a 2-5 game and got seated pretty quickly. Thankfully it wasn't at Sophie's table. I was pretty sure Falcon and Golden Guy were over from Houston and I had no interest in messing with them. It had been a while since I had sat down at a poker table. I had spent many nights in underground rooms in Houston, but stopped going when a gang of Asians with Uzis started hitting the rooms. Had no interest in being there when that happened. Besides, we had been on such a ridiculous roll at the track, I had not really even thought about poker. But here I was, back in my element. I bought in for $1,000, noticing several large stacks. There were nine players, and four had stacks well over $1,000.

In a 2-5 game, two players are required to put up money. The small blind ($2) and the big blind ($5). It doesn't sound like a lot of money, but pots can grow very fast, especially in a no-limit game, which is what we were playing. No-Limit Hold 'Em was all anyone played anymore, especially in casinos. I was always partial to 7-card stud, but good luck finding that game anywhere. In reality, this was like a 2-5-10 game, because there was a "straddle" every hand, where the first person to act could automatically post double the blinds. A couple times we even had double straddles.

I sat the first few minutes observing. The player to my left was hyper aggressive. He had about $1,500 in chips, and was firing at every pot, chasing away almost everyone. He was the player I was going to go after. Cash games are about patience. Waiting for a hand or a situation where you can score big. Small pots are OK, but the key to making money in these games is to take down a couple monster pots. The more chips you have, the more aggressive you can be, which is what the guy next to me was doing.

He was about my age, Hispanic, wearing a Dallas Cowboys hat and a Troy Aikman jersey. I know it sounds racist, but Asians and Mexicans were usually the most aggressive players. They loved to gamble. You had to be careful to not get drawn in with a marginal hand with players like that, or your chips would disappear fast. Sometimes you might have to wait as long as an hour. This night it was the fifth hand, about 10 minutes in. Cowboy fan had played every hand since I had been at the table. On this particular hand, I was the big blind, with $5 already invested. He straddled for $10. By the time the action got to me, four other players had called the $10. I looked down to 7-9 of spades, a hand I had no problem tossing in another $5 so I could see a flop. But Cowboy wasn't going to let us in cheap. He immediately raised it to $40. It was the tactic he had been employing all along; let the others limp in, then bet them off their chips. Only this time, no one went away. When it got to me, all four had called. There was already over $200 in the pot, and for an additional $30, I would be playing for it. It was an easy call. My strategy was simple. If I miss the flop, I fold. If I catch enough to hang around, I see how the betting goes and calculate my odds. If I hit it hard, I reel them in.

The flop could not have been better for me. 6 of spades, 10 of diamonds, 8 of clubs. I had flopped the nut straight. Now I just hoped one of them hit, and I could milk the hand for as much money as possible. I was first to act, and checked. I wanted to look weak. Cowboy bet $70. It was kind of an odd bet. It was less than a third of the pot. A good player might do that to set off some alarm bells with the other players. I was hoping the others would see through it and hang around. Only one did. An old, graying lady with glasses and a constant scowl was on the button (the last to act). She made the call. So did I.

The turn was what we call a blank, the 2 of hearts. It's not a card that could have realistically helped any of us. Of course, I didn't need the help. I checked again. This time, Cowboy made it $150 to go. Granny stalled, looking at her hand a couple times. My guess was she had top pair with a so-so kicker, something like J-10. She had seen Cowboy be aggressive, and was pretty sure she had him beat. She wasn't even thinking about me. Granny made the call, as did I. I had more than 1/4th of my chips in the pot now. The goal was to get them all in.

I did not know it right away, but the last card was going to help me do just that. The ace of spades hit on the river. There was literally nothing on the board that could beat my straight. What worried me is it might scare off Cowboy and Granny if I bet. The ace was a scare card. There was more money to be made, so I had to make it look like I was afraid of the ace. So once again, I checked. Cowboy quickly threw out 200 chips. The ace did scare Granny away. She disgustingly folded. I had been right. She had J10 or Q10. The ace was not what she wanted to see. Too bad. But now I hoped Cowboy had the ace. I re-raised, but only to $400. My thinking was if he had something weak, it might be a small enough bet to induce him to call. Also, I only had $340 left after the bet and he might think I was trying to hang on to a few chips and shove me off it the bet. In the end, all that thinking didn't matter. He shoved all in, and I called. He had A-10 and had hit two pair on the river. I was pretty sure he said "motherfucker" in Spanish when he saw my hand.

I raked over $2k on that pot, more than doubling up, and gave the dealer a nice tip. I would play for two more hours, and cash out for over $5,000. I could have played longer, but by then the alcohol was turning me into a zombie again, and I knew I needed sleep. And after I cleaned Cowboy out a second time, it was time to head to the hotel. He had built his stack back up nicely, and we had not butted heads since the first hand. The other big one I won was with pocket aces vs. granny's pocket kings, so Cowboy had only seen me show two hands all night. A nut straight and aces. I announced this was my last hand before it was dealt. The idea was if I caught something good, it would look like I was hanging around simply because it was my last hand. It only worked about one time in 20. This was the one.

I was on the button with pocket 4s. There was a $10 straddle. I raised to $50, and Cowboy immediately made it $100 from the small blind. The big blind and straddle folded, and I called. Already $215 in the pot. The flop was one you dream of hitting. 4-4-7. Boom. Quads. Ordinarily I would check, but I wanted Cowboy to think I was just trying to take the pot, so I led out for $200. He had gone all-in instantly for all $1,200 of his chips. I snap called, and he flipped over pocket queens. I was called a lot worse things this time around.

This was what I had been missing. At the track, we had lost the possibility of losing. It took away the joy of winning. Here, at this table, in this dirty casino where I was afraid to touch the chips for fear of getting leprosy...this is why I gambled. I might do everything right and lose. I might do everything wrong and win. But it was going to be one or the other. And it was going to be based on decisions I made. And I would never have been able to explain this to Jen, but this was my reason for living. This is what I wanted to do. Sit at a poker table for the rest of my life.

But then, I was pretty drunk. I did not think I could walk the four blocks to the hotel. I cashed out, caught a cab, barely conscious at this point. But I felt good. $5,000 was nothing compared to what we had made at the track. But this had been all me. I was proud. I don't remember getting back to the room, but somehow I did.

When I woke up the next morning, I had that weird feeling I had done something stupid. I usually did when I was blackout drunk. But when I found my pants on the floor loaded with black chips, I started piecing the night back together. As always, I made sure I had my wallet, phone and keys. I showered, got dressed, and went to the bar for a screwdriver. For me, screwdrivers and margaritas were the perfect hangover cures. They were even better when you were still drunk from the night before. Enough alcohol to balance yourself, enough sugar and other crap to soak in the alcohol. As long as you just had a couple. More than that, and you were right back on the train.

It was a little after 11, and I had planned to play the 11 a.m. poker tournament, but I had needed the sleep. I was feeling pretty good. I had missed a few texts from Sophie, who had done very well at the poker table as well. Apparently she took a couple big pots off her old nemesis in Houston, the Falcon. He had been a dick about it. Made her happy. I also had a couple from Jen. I told her I was not going to take the job in New Orleans, that I did not want to leave Houston, did not want to leave her. I did not need to keep reeling her in. She was a trout, caught, flopping on the deck. But I was enjoying it. And part of me was thinking that buying a place together downtown would be terrific. Big enough so we would not be in each other's faces all the time. And as long as she was working during the day…well, she did not have to know if I hit a poker room or two.

I was enjoying some time to myself, taking in the sights in the French Quarter. The freak shows were already out. Before Katrina, the French Quarter was a charming place, but a little seedy. Since then, it had just become seedy. Usually when I came here now I only spent the first day around the Quarter. The rest of the time I would hit Frenchmen Street. Wandering around Bourbon Street at night really wasn't fun anymore. The pros would come up to you in the middle of the street. On the outskirts, hookers would try to pick you up in their cars. And yes, that would get you robbed in a hurry. It was muggy and hot, and I went to Mother's for a big breakfast. Between that and the screwdriver, my body was balancing out yesterday's abuse. Oddly, I was still hungry, so I hit Acme for some grilled oysters. Since I was by myself, I did not have to wait in line very long. I had not been eating much lately, but today I was ravenous. And the food is so good in New Orleans. And yeah, these were touristy places, but fuck it. Today I was a tourist.

Finally, I made my way to the casino, not sure what I was going to do. That got answered right away, when Jesse and Michael, sitting at the bar, spotted me. We chatted for a bit. Apparently they had killed it at blackjack the night before. Jesse had some "system" that was paying off. They were about to go again. Jesse said it worked better with three people, and asked if I had 10k to play with. "Got a little over five in chips from poker last night," I said. "I could go to the bank and get more." But Jesse just said he would stake the other half. I was OK with it. I hated blackjack. I always stayed with games where it was me against other humans -- poker, horse racing, sports betting. When it's me against the house? Well, there is a reason they have those giant casinos and I live in a one-bedroom apartment.

Apparently they had done well enough the night before that there was a private blackjack table waiting for us with a $100 minimum. Most of the tables had $10 minimums this time of day on a Thursday. We also had our own private drink girl, who kept them coming every five minutes. We each started with 10k, and basically did everything Jesse said. I don't know enough about blackjack to give you the details of how we did it. Jesse would just tell us what to do, all the time staring at the cards and deck. I had heard of counting cards, but I did not know how it worked. I knew it was legal, but frowned on. Then again, casinos only frown if you win.

And boy, did we win. My $10k quickly became 80. Jesse was over 200. And that was in an hour. By hour two, we were completely lit, and between the three of us had nearly $700k on the table. Drink girl got a $1,000 tip. Jesse was too drunk to notice, and Michael was too caught up in it, but I started getting that creepy, nervous feeling that I had at the track before James came around. And two well- dressed men with ear pieces were watching us, the same venom I had seen in James' eyes. It was about that time the pit boss came over. "Gentlemen, why don't you take a break? I will get your chips racked up and brought to you. Here are some passes to the VIP room in the steak house. Dinner's on us." Jesse was drunk enough now that he did not want to stop. "I don't need a break..." The pit boss, was short, wide, half Italian, half Cajun, all no-nonsense. "I insist." Michael knew what that meant. "Let's go, fellas. I could use a steak."

Michael did not really want a steak. None of us did. I was still stuffed, and Jesse was sloppy now. When the pit boss brought our money, he had the two security guards with him. He did not look happy. "So this is a pretty big score for you guys..." Jesse was so drunk he was about to pass out. Michael was on point as usual, though, and took over. Besides, they spoke the same language. "Look, our guy here is really good. It was a nice run. We are willing to lose some back. In fact, we might even donate some back just for this nice VIP treatment you are giving us." It wasn't really a VIP room. It was a private room where they did private business. Like us. "That won't be necessary," he said. "We are just going to ask you to leave. Don't come back. And we've put out the word to every other casino in Louisiana." Jesse popped up. "We didn't do anything wrong." Pit Boss smiled, and it was scary. "Be that as it may, you guys have to know how this works."

"So we can't win here," Jesse said. "There's winning," the pit boss said, "and there's this. You get to do this once. But you don't get to come back. That simple." Michael spoke up. "Thank you. We will cash out and get out of here. Let's go boys. We have dinner plans anyway." He pulled a rack worth $300,000 and gave it to the pit boss. "For your favorite charity or whatever. Or back to the house. We don't want any hard feelings." The pit boss took it without a word. Michael knew the game. This was a tribute, a payoff to get them to leave everybody alone. It was how Michael's world worked, and Michael had thought that would be the end of it. He was dead wrong. We met the others in a back room at an old, fancy restaurant, the kind where the waiter gives you a long soliloquy about the history of the place. There were pictures of famous people. The one that stood out was Bing Crosby. It reminded me of the old Balinese Room in Galveston. I missed that place.

I wish I could remember the name of the restaurant. Something like Angelo's. I don't really know. I had never seen Jesse so drunk. The place only served wine and beer, and Jesse ordered several bottles of merlot.

He had already killed one off when we sat down. The food was amazing, and everyone was in a good mood. They had no idea how nervous Jesse, Michael and I were. Drunkenly, Jesse toasted everyone.

"You might have figured this out, but we don't have much time left together." The mood suddenly turned sour. "I love every one of you. And you all have something important to do when this is all over. You will know what it is." I couldn't help myself. "Even me?" Jesse laughed. He was loud talking now, the alcohol consuming him. "You most of all, Louis. Different, yes. But it's important. The most important." He came over and hugged me. "You were always my favorite." We spent the rest of the night drinking, telling stories, jokes, enjoying each other's company as a group for what would be the last time. It was sad, but it was beautiful, poignant. A group of misfit friends who started as gambling degenerates and now were having a $10,000 dinner in a ritzy restaurant in New Orleans. I was pretty drunk now, too, when it hit me, and I had to laugh at myself. *The Last Supper.* I didn't know much about the real last supper, other than it was a painting. I try to imagine what they were all thinking then. My group was different. They were happy. Even though it was all ending, we all knew it had to. That there was another life for all of us. Another destiny. And it was Mare who was slowly taking charge. Making plans.

Talking about the next few days. Mare was the new leader. We could all see that clear as day. Strong, powerful Mare. I wasn't feeling the whole end of it all thing. I knew we could never go back to the track, but some of the people would always be friends. Maybe Michael most of all.

And I had already planned to move on, so it really wasn't a big deal. My only issue now was what to do with Sophie and what was presumably my kid. And, oh yeah, Jen. I might have gone too far with that ruse. But then part of me wanted to. In the worst way. I had confused my shit more than ever. Jesse passed out briefly, and everybody laughed. When he came to, he asked Michael, Mare and me to stay for a moment. Hugs were exchanged. Pete gave me a big kiss. Goodbyes were said. Plans were made. A bunch were going on a ghost tour tomorrow. Others were hitting the casino again. One group was going to the Fair Grounds for simulcasting.

When they left, Jesse settled the bill, first ordering us all very strong coffee. "I need a favor, guys," Jesse said. We just nodded. The coffee was too late to save all of us. "Louis, you need to write this story. I know you have been doing it anyway. But it needs to be told." I nodded. I had been taking notes, but had yet to actually do any writing. "Michael has something for you. His story. Will you work it in?" Now I was intrigued. I knew there had to be more good stuff in there. "Of course. Probably more interesting than my stuff," I said.

Michael handed me a handwritten notebook. Jesse laughed again. "Mare has been journaling, too. She will give hers to Sophie in the morning. Does that work for you?" I still had that brief resentment of taking orders, but I quietly agreed.

"Good," he said. "Meet me and Michael out front of the hotel at 10. We're going to play golf. We can buy clothes and rent clubs when we get there. I will tell you what is up then." Again, we nodded. "Let's get out of here," he said. "I need to pass out."

Sophie was waiting for me outside, and we quietly went to my room and had rough, drunken sex. It was as good as I ever remembered. It reminded me of the old days with Jen. I woke up about an hour later, drunker than I have ever been. The world was spinning, like when I was younger and drunk for the first time. There were tiny flowers on the hotel wall, but when I tried to focus, they were constantly in motion, like millions of marching ants. I made it to the commode just in time to throw up in about seven different colors. I had not thrown up from drinking in years. I think it was the wine. That crap always did me in. I slept on the bathroom floor most of the night, occasionally waking up to hurl again. It felt like my college days. About 7:30 I woke up, showered, and felt relatively normal again. I mixed a screwdriver from the mini bar, downed it quickly, and suddenly felt much better.

Sophie was waiting for me in bed. I could see the beginnings of a bump on her otherwise flat stomach. We made love again and then curled up in silence. Finally, she spoke. "Louis, I'm going home today.

With Mare. We have some things to plan out."

For some reason, I was expecting this. "OK, that sounds good." More silence. Then I started recalling some of the things from last night. "Hey, can you do me a favor?" She smiled, also expecting it. "Like, of course." I don't know when or why I had formulated this plan, but it all made sense. "I need you to take some things back for me. I have some writing to do. My laptop, a notebook from Michael, and a journal Mare is going to give you today." She pulled herself close to me. "Sure."

"Take them to my condo in Galveston. I'll write down the address and I have an extra key I will leave you. When I get back, I'm going to lock down and write this, and that's the best place to do it. As soon as you can get it there, OK? I'll be there in a couple days."

"What happens when you are, like, done?" She asked. I thought long and hard. "Sophie, I don't know what will happen with you and me. But I want to be part of our kid's life either way. I want to be a real father this time." She smiled. "I want that to. And as far as us...let's just keep playing it by ear, OK? Like that seems to work." We chatted a while longer, and I started sounding more and more like a responsible adult. Well, except for the other woman I was telling the same things. I could hear Jen's voice. "You've changed, Louis." The fuck I have. Little Paul had drawn up a will for me. It only made sense. I gave it to Sophie and explained some things. "So I have trust funds set up for my other kids. And if anything happens to me, all the rest is split between a friend of mine and you and the kid." She smiled.

"I don't, like, need it," she said. "And nothing is going to happen to you."

"I know that," I said. "But I drink a lot. You never know." She looked it over. "Who is Gennara Haddad?" I was flushed a little, but I had gotten really good at lying again. "My old boss. She kept me employed when I should have been fired. They pay her shit wages. Anything ever happens

I want her to have a nice life." Sophie pulled herself tightly against me again. "You are a good man, Louis." And I had the oddest feeling. After years of being overly emotional, borderline schizo, worried about everything...At 43 years old, finally I was growing up. I was starting to realize that some things just did not matter. Sophie and Jesse? Who cares? Hell, that could have been me, Jesse and Mare on another night. And yes, more than ever I was convinced Jesse was just a con man who fixed races and counted cards. Who cared? Look how much money he had made me. Wondering about the how was foolish. I had everything I could possibly want. I did not think I needed a second chance at being a father, but I was glad to have one. I was going to be around for this kid. Watch him or her grow. Hopefully get an athlete this time.

And I had hope things could work out with Sophie. She was changing, too. Maybe both of us changing would take us to a place where we could be happy. If not? I really think the thing with Jen could work. I could be happy there, too. Wow, I really was thinking marriage again. Jen? Sophie? Nobody? Somebody else? Heck, guess part of me was growing up a little. We chatted a while longer, and I helped Sophie pack up her stuff and mine. Mare dropped off her notebook, which I carefully put with everything else. It was all there. My life. Everyone's lives. And I trusted Sophie with it. Completely. We said our goodbyes, with a renewed hope for the future. I gave her one last hug and felt her tight little body against me. I savored that moment, knowing that it was special. I did not know then it was the last time I would ever see her. And I would never see my future child.

That was happening a lot. To all of us. I don't know what I would have said or done differently. Do you really tell someone you are never going to see them again? In truth, I didn't know at the time. I really thought I would spend more time with Jen. With Sophie. With Michael. With everybody. Even if I could have lived with what happened to Jesse -- and maybe, just maybe I could have forgiven myself at some point -- what happened on the boat would end all hope. I wish I had known. I wish I had told Sophie and Jen I loved them, in person, one last time. I guess this will have to do.

One thing I liked about all of us; for all the drinking, a day later we were always fresh as though we had never taken a drink. Jesse looked like a million bucks. Michael half a million. They had been there early, talking about God knows what. They greeted me warmly, and Jesse was on his way to the cab stand when a black SUV pulled up. The window rolled down, and the Pit Boss smiled. "We will give you guys a ride." I panicked, but Jesse and even Michael seemed OK, and walked to the back doors. All that Zen I had built up washed away in a second. "What the hell are we doing, Jesse?" He smiled.

"Don't worry. They just want to talk." I could not help but worry. In fact, it was all I could do. And I wasn't just worried. I was flat out scared.

BOOK 16: THE GOSPEL ACCORDING TO MARE CHAPTER 3

We both passed out in our room after making it back from the restaurant. About 3:00 a.m. I was awakened by Jesse's hardness gently rubbing against my ass, and I willingly woke up and climbed on top of him. It was transcendent. I could not stop cumming. Afterward, Jesse started spilling out instructions. On life, parenting, everything. I listened patiently, then finally started getting angry. "You sound like you aren't going to be here, Jess. Your daughter needs her father." He smiled at me. I always melted at that smile. Who didn't? "No matter what, she will always have her father. Besides, her mother is more than enough."

He reminded me to give my journal to Louis. I objected briefly -- it was hard to trust Louis -- but Jesse insisted. "He's a writer," Jesse said. "He will tell your story. You know all those people we've reached? Imagine what a book could do. Imagine the people we could touch..." I was still hung over, and I wasn't buying it. And I just wanted to climb back on top of him again. He laughed. "I understand, believe me. Louis is a mess. Always has been. But that's his role in this. Tell the story. Let people draw their own conclusions. Isn't that what we are about?" I nodded. "It's always going to be dangerous, Mare. But you are stronger than any of us. You will be the one they flock to. And you should be."

I had to admit, I was embracing that. I was ready for it. Jesse had made me ready. I suspected he would be going away for a while, but I knew he would be back. I knew I had been asked to do something special. To help change the world. To do wonderful things. To have those faces staring at me for my message. To see them transform. When Jesse had said in the sermon at the bar that making people money made him happy, I understood. What made me happy was seeing those faces. Seeing the realization. The learning. The change. There is nothing more beautiful in this world than a mind coming to life. Maybe even a soul. Seeing the lights come on. Seeing people find commonality. Smart, stupid, rich, poor. Seeing them all look at me and see the same thing. Hear the same message. To see them change, transform. To learn to care about everyone, not just themselves. That is what made me happiest.

We all had something different like that, and I believe Jesse brought it out of all of us. He truly was special. His greatest gift was not that he made a bunch of people a ridiculous amount of money. He taught a small few of us a truth that could change the world. And it became our goal to do just that. There is a lot of speculation on who Jesse was, and he wanted you to decide that for yourself, just like I did. My decision was easy. As the woman who loved him most, and the mother of his child, I believe Jesse was -- and is -- the Jesus of his time.

BOOK 17: THE GOSPEL ACCORDING TO LOUIS CHAPTER 10

The ride in the SUV was the longest of my life. I don't think we went very far -- maybe 50 miles -- but it seemed to take forever. Pit Boss had frisked us, and taken Michael's gun. He asked when he did it -- "do you always take a gun to the golf course? Michael replied with a smile. "I take a gun everywhere." Pit Boss snorted in admiration.

It was way too cold in the SUV. The air conditioner was turned up full blast. I felt a chill all the way to my soul. Had our greed finally caught up with us? Was taking the casino's money the final step too far in a string of overly greedy decisions? Again, I blamed Jesse. There was no need to hit the casino that hard. No need. But we had done it anyway. Michael broke the silence. "Any chance we can get some drinks?" Pit Boss smiled his dumb smile, and poured us Jack on the rocks. He had one himself. "To winning," he said. I felt awkward toasting that.

All I could think of was the life that waited for me. Sophie. Our kid. Writing books. Hanging at the beach. Watching the sun set over Galveston Bay. I could hear Sophie saying it was "like, beautiful." Or maybe Jen, penthouse apartment, her reading some story I had written and critically going over everything she hated. Or dead in the back of this SUV because somebody got too fucking greedy. I wondered who would tell our story now. If I was gone, my notes would not make sense to anyone else. If Jesse were truly special, I would have to survive this, because no one else could write it. I saw the whole story in my head to that point. From the first day Jesse showed up, to the first big score, to making love to Sophie. I couldn't see the end, though. I suspected that was coming.

Michael and Pit Boss were having a cordial conversation about hand guns and range vs. firepower. Jesse was just smiling, like he had a secret that we all knew but were afraid to admit it. For some reason, I remembered being a little kid, innocent, having done nothing wrong yet. I was about four -- it was one of my first memories. Our cat had kittens, and I loved them. One day, I threw one in the pool to watch it swim. I didn't know cats could not swim. The kitten drowned, and my mom was furious. I felt terrible. I didn't know. We had a really fat teacher in fourth grade. In retrospect, I think he was gay in a time when it wasn't cool to be gay. We teased him mercilessly. Said all sorts of terrible things. When the year was over, he asked me to stay after class. I thought he was going to flunk me, tell me what a terrible kid I was. He didn't. He said I was his favorite student, and he hoped I would someday learn that being nice to people would only make me better. He said I had talent. I remember breaking down and crying and apologizing for all the mean things. All he said was, "every kid does that. You know why you were my favorite? You realized it was wrong." He died from a heart attack a year later.

I remembered my first time, in a swimming pool in Galveston. I was 12. We were so high. It was my friend's girlfriend. We started kissing in the pool. Before I knew it, she had slid me inside her and taken off her bathing suit bottom. I didn't last very long and had no clue what I was

185

doing. I never saw her again and the friend never spoke to me again. My first real girlfriend was when I was 15. Darla, I was driving then (I wasn't supposed to be). We met at the beach and made love in the water. I really thought she was the one. Two days later I went to pick her up on a date at the Yacht Basin, and her rich ass father came out and told me to disappear and never come around again. His daughter was never going out with white trash. White trash. That stayed with me a long time.

A few weeks later, I was supposed to be hanging out at the beach with some friends. I begged out at the last minute, deciding to go fishing instead. It was one of those times where I wanted to be alone. I was missing Darla. My friends crashed their truck on a dune that night, and everyone in the back -- where I would have been -- was thrown out. One kid died. Another was paralyzed. It could have been me. Fronting my first band, the Dangles. Singing Sympathy for the Devil. Bringing the house down. The girl from high school, Sabrina Red. She was not attractive. Not ugly, just no one you would notice. Pale, really thin, bruised easily, never went to gym class, looked way too young for high school. I was holding court with my cool kid friends at lunch. I was editor of the paper. Lead singer of The Dangles. I was as cool as I would ever be. Sabrina, who had never said a word to anyone that we knew of, came up and asked if she could talk to me. She had a story for me. But I was so cool. I told her I would be in touch.

I finally was, two weeks later, when I visited her at County Hospital. Turns out those bruises were from her dad. He had been beating her and raping her for years. She had looked up to me, admired me, wanted me to tell the story. I did. It won every possible award. A year later I took her on a date, and apologized for not listening right away. She told me it was OK. No one listened. It took her dad crossing the line and doing that much damage to get people to notice. To listen. He was in jail for 25 years. She was coping. I fell in love with her, but she went to school in Germany and I never saw her again. I think she wanted to get away from me as much as him. Drunk in a bar with my best friend from high school. He was just back from Iraq. He had been special forces in the first Gulf War. Trained sniper whose only mission was to shadow an Iraqi general. He would check in every four hours, waiting for one of three orders: Stand down, stay on mission, green.

For a week it was stay on mission. He followed the man everywhere. Watched him take his kids to soccer practice. Saw him with his mistress. Saw him give coins to kids in the street. Got to know him. Then one day, he got a new order. Green. He did not hesitate. But they never thought about what it would do to him. What it was like to know someone that well and have to kill them. He drank himself to death within a year of returning home and telling that story. Damned shame.

That night in the garage with Jen. The look on Paula's face, one of anger and maybe relief. The betrayal. I had been so stupid. We could have carried on for months and no one would have ever known. And I think that's what pissed Paula off the most. We had done it right under her nose, flaunting it. With our friends 20 feet away. The arrogance it took. Paula never let me see the kids again. That mole, staring at me once again. That fucking mole. Then finally a night in Tijuana outside a whore house, where a man put a knife to my throat and stole all my cash. He was going to slit my throat, but somebody showed up at the last second. I was supposed to die there, ingloriously. And for some reason, that particular memory gave me comfort, because no matter what happened, I wasn't supposed to be here. Everything since had been a bonus. So whatever happened now would not matter. I noticed Jesse looking at me, and for some reason I was smiling too. I don't think you are ever more alive than when death is watching over your shoulder.

I laughed out loud, and Pit Boss looked at me like I was crazy. Maybe I was. I was ready for whatever he had planned. At least I thought I was. Hell, I thought I was going to die. That would have been easy.

BOOK 18: THE GOSPEL ACCORDING TO LOUIS CHAPTER 11

They had taken us to a place on the water. I am not sure what it was. It seemed like an abandoned warehouse next to a dock for a shrimp boat. We weren't in New Orleans anymore, but I had no idea where it was. I guessed we were still in Louisiana, but maybe Mississippi. I had not paid attention during the trip. Regardless, there was no one in the area. I could tell this was a part of the country that had been devastated by Katrina, and clearly no one had come back. No one but us. They handcuffed us to three chairs and lined us up against a wall, Jesse in between us. It was the Pit Boss and his two security guards. We could hear another man moving around outside. Pit Boss was all business. "So we will make this easy. Just answer my questions and we will get you to your golf game. Fair enough?"

We nodded. "Good. We know you are cheating. I need to know how. I can't have the casino get hit like that again. I'm willing to let it all go, but I need to know how. Was the dealer in on it?" We looked at Jesse. He spoke, quietly. "The dealer was not in on it. Remember, we went through three of them. No way we could have gotten to all three."

Pit Boss looked thoughtful. "OK, then. How?" Jesse smiled. "I know you don't want to hear this, but we weren't cheating." He sighed. "I've looked at the tape. Every move was perfect. That's not realistic. Just tell me. No one wants to do this. We just want to tighten up security. You

189

just want to play golf. Easy fix." No one said anything. One of the security guards turned on some music. It was The End by the Doors. Michael asked if he could talk to someone called "Johnny Fives." The Pit Boss smiled. "Mr. Rossi is too busy for something like this."

"He would make time for me," Michael said. The Pit Boss pulled Michael's weapon and pointed it at him. "Just who the fuck are you?" Jesse interrupted. "Let it go, Michael. There's nothing we can say to change their minds."

"No?" Said the Pit Boss. "Well I gotta shoot one of you now so maybe the others will talk." "NO!" I screamed. "Do not shoot. He was counting cards. That's it. Surely you have dealt with that before." The Pit Boss looked somewhat satisfied. "Counting cards? This guy, right?" He pointed the gun at Jesse. I nodded solemnly. I could feel the music now. *"He took a face from the ancient gallery and he walked on down the hall..."* I realized I had fucked up. If I had just kept my mouth shut, maybe we talk our way out of this. I had just thought if we gave them something they would let us go.

"OK," Pit Boss said. "He dies. You two live. Easy enough." He pulled the trigger, but Michael had reacted quickly. He jumped in front of Jesse, and the bullet struck him in the chest. He hit the ground in a heap, his chair clanging. Jesse wept. Michael wasn't dead yet. He was smiling. He motioned the pit boss over with his head. "What, now you got something to say?" Michael whispered something in his ear. The fat pit boss turned white. "Fuck! The fuck you didn't say anything?" Michael just looked at me, smiling. He said something I didn't understand at the time, but after reading his journal, it made perfect sense. "Thirty one," he had said. And then I watched my friend, the man I had spent so much time with, the man who was the worst of us, die before my eyes, smiling. Taking a bullet for Jesse. And suddenly I knew who Jesse was. And I finally believed. And Michael had done the one thing that would get him back to even in life. And I had finally committed my great sin. My friend was dead because of me. I had called Jesse out as a card counter. This was likely the end for him, too. Me. Louis, who was just a bad person. Now I was truly evil.

The Pit Boss grabbed his bald head and looked scared. He had called Mr. Rossi, who was on his way. Apparently at the end Michael had told him who he really was. And that was bad news for Pit Boss. Jesse just sat quietly, mumbling something that sounded like prayer. We sat there like that for about 20 minutes, until in walked a perfectly dressed, extremely handsome Italian man with a wide-brimmed fedora. He took one look at Michael and turned on the Pit Boss.

"How the fuck does this happen? Do you know how fucked we are?" The Pit Boss was scared, stammering. "I swear, boss, he didn't say a word. He asked to talk to you, but he didn't say why or who he was. And it was accident. I was trying to shoot this piece of shit (he pointed at Jesse) but Scraps took a bullet for him. Rossi walked around in circles, then took the gun. He stood behind Jesse, placed the gun in Jesse's hand, and put another bullet in Michael. He looked at me with a dark stare that seemed to see through every fiber of my soul. "You, pay attention," he said to me. "You are the one who came clean, right?" I nodded. "OK, everybody, so this is how it played out. The card counter here shot his friend in the alley behind the casino while some homeless was trying to rob them. Go find a homeless and put a bullet in him. These three were drunk, it was an accident. You guys found them, and realized who he killed. So we took care of him. This guy saw the whole thing. None of us were anywhere near this." He looked directly at me. "And that's the story you tell when they ask. And they will fucking ask."

I nodded, but I was sick to my stomach. There was no way I could tell that story. He seemed to know that. "Don't worry, I've got some insurance. You won't have any problems remembering." He turned to the security guards. "Get Boudreaux. Take these two out on the boat. That one (pointing to Jesse again) gets nailed to the mast. He dies slow."

He looked at me again, satisfaction on his face. "This one gets the Boudreaux treatment. And after that, if he doesn't tell the story exactly the way we say? He spends the rest of his life on Boudreaux's boat." He came over, close to me, smelling of old spice. There was something attractive about him. I found it an odd thought at the time.

"You are gonna wish we killed you, snitch. But you will get through it. And when you do, just remember, tell anybody a story other than what I just said, and what happens to you will happen every day for the rest of your miserable fucking life. Tell the story right and you walk away from this." Then he laughed. "Well, maybe not walk..." The others laughed as well. I did not find their secret amusing. He pointed to Michael's body. "His people...They are going to be tough on you when they ask what happened. Get you to say something else. No matter what they do, it will never be worse than Boudreaux's boat. Don't forget that."

I nodded. It didn't matter anymore. I was dead. I knew it. It all came down to how and when. Rossi ordered one of the men to clean up Michael's body and get it to his people in Houston. "We have to look like the good guys here," he said. Everyone wanted me to tell a story. Jesse. Now this Rossi character. The difference is, Jesse wanted the truth. These guys wanted fiction. Well, I was always a lot better at truth, so that is how it happened. Should someone find this, and pass on to Michael's friends what actually occurred, so be it. That story of theirs was a fucking joke anyway. And I am not afraid of going back to Boudreaux's boat. I will be dead before they find out anyway. The man who finished this? Louis? Me? A man who suddenly had things he wanted to live for just a few days before? He died on that boat.

The shrimp boat was just outside. I had no idea what was in store for me, but I was broken. My friend was dead. Jesse was about to be dead because I gave him up. And with everything I had seen, I was now convinced Jesse was no con man at all, but as Mare would call him, "the Jesus of his time." I was dead. I accepted that. The only plan I had was to try to stay alive long enough to let Michael's friends know what really happened. No matter what happened on Boudreaux's boat, I would not be coming back. I would be long dead. Hell, Michael's friends might do it for me. But I wanted to stay alive long enough to make right what I could. But I also knew I probably was never getting off that boat alive. That everything would have been for nothing anyway.

I thought of all the things I could have done differently in my life. And the one thing I wish I had back had just happened. Jesse had taken away the other's pain from their past mistakes. But now here I was, with the worst mistake of all, and Jesse was going to be gone. I wish I had just said "I was counting cards." Taken the fall. Then Jesse and Michael would be alive. And I would be gone, without having to go on Boudreaux's boat. Jesse and I were still cuffed. His head was down, and he had not said a word. "I'm sorry, Jess," I said. "I should have taken the fall." He smiled at me. "Tell the story. You know the truth now. This was your destiny all along. Just like taking the fall was mine. Just like taking that bullet was Michael's."

"Jesse...did you set all this up?" He smiled at me. "Just tell the story." I wasn't sure I bought that. I think he was trying to make me feel better. I did not know what was going to happen to me on that boat, but I suspect he did. And apparently he was going to get off easier than I was. A fat, greasy pig of a man with a matted beard and overalls with no shirt underneath waddled towards us. He was talking to Pit Boss in pure Cajun, almost impossible to understand. So this was Boudreaux. They took Jesse first as they fired up the engine. Pit Boss' men nailed him to the mast, arms spread. We were going out to sea. The heat and the blood loss would kill him in a few hours at most. But it would not be quick. Jesse Christian, the Jesus of our time, was going to die crucified on a dirty shrimp boat, with the cackles of sea gulls -- rats with wings -- overhead.

They brought me on board, still cuffed. The others left, and Boudreaux took us out in the Gulf of Mexico, presumably in an area no one else would go. It was suffocatingly hot. My shirt was drenched in five minutes. The heat from the boat's engine only made it worse. And my god this boat stunk of dead fish, diesel and sweat. The fat man didn't talk much. After about 20 minutes, Boudreaux came for me. "In dere, bitch," he pointed to the cabin. I took one last look at Jesse. The boat was loud, the wind was roaring, the seagulls screaming...but I thought I heard Jesse say "Eli, Eli, Llama Sabatchthani." I would not see him again.

Boudreaux slammed me against the wall, and I passed out. When I came to, my pants were off, and suddenly I understood. Boudreaux had his pants down. He was jacking off, using grease from the engine. His dick was giant. He was smiling at me. He finally spoke, in his deep Cajun accent. "Mouf or azz, bitch?" I did not understand. "MOUF OR AZZ, BITCH!" *Mouth or ass.* Oh shit. He had just wanted me to realize what was going to happen to me. And then he spoke, and I felt chills, even in the interminable heat. "Bofe, Boudreaux say…"

The cabin was greasy, dirty. There was a little fake alligator on the wheel, which had been tied to keep us on the same course. The chunk, click, chunk, click of the engine created a dirty rhythm. The boat was swaying from the waves, side to side in rhythm. Sometimes a bigger wave would come along and make it worse. I tried to struggle, but the man was huge, powerful. He had his arm around my throat, enough to daze me without rendering me unconscious. He wanted me awake for this. And suddenly, I felt like someone had shoved a baseball bat all the way up my ass and hit me in the chest. Boudreaux shoved again, harder this time. It was more than pain. It was as if I was being stabbed in the ass by a giant knife. And then he was in full stride, shoving into me, harder and harder each time. He was slamming me now, laughing the whole time.

"You like dat Boudreaux's bitch? You like dat big azz Boudreaux dick?" Suddenly there was a knife at my throat. "You pazz out, you trow up, you die." The entire boat seemed to be shaking, all from Boudreaux's thrusts. I was completely helpless. All I could do was wish it would end soon. But it didn't. It was at least 10 minutes in when I felt something running down my legs. Maybe blood. Maybe my own shit. Maybe grease. Maybe all three. I was about to find out. "Mouf time, Boudreaux say." He pulled out, placed the knife at my throat, and said, "you trow up, you bite, Boudreaux feed you to sharks."

And then it was in my mouth, and I tasted all three. Blood. My own shit. Grease. I tried to gag, but I knew he would kill me. So I just did the best I could to block out the taste. And then I felt the squirt of greasy cum shooting down my throat. "Swallow all of it," he said.

"Good lil bitch." He left it there for another minute or two before I could finally breathe again. He slammed me down. "Boudreaux be back soon." I was completely broken at that point. My legs were completely numb, my throat ripped, my stomach retching. I lay on the floor, swaying with the waves. Rossi was right. I wished I was dead. Meanwhile, somewhere above me, Jesse probably already was. As bad as it was, I would have been OK. Except Boudreaux did his thing three more times that day, each longer and more violent than the one before. Once, he shoved a wrench up my ass, then a fish, all while he jacked it, spraying in my face. He talked the whole time in his disgusting Cajun accent. Telling me how I was his bitch. How much I was enjoying it. How he wanted me here every day. How he had so much more planned for me. Finally, after the last time, I threw up, just missing him. He knocked me out cold.

I dreamed of dragons, sharks, mermaids. The water, always so friendly, was mean. Dangerous. Dark. I had always loved the water. But now all I could see was danger. And now I was in my tub, the water blood red again. I woke up in my room at the hotel. My first thought is the whole thing was a dream, and I needed to get up and meet Jesse and Michael for golf. But then I felt the unbearable pain in my rectum, tasted the disgust in my throat. And I realized, it had all been real. I could barely stand up, but I made my way to the bathroom, and brushed my teeth for a good ten minutes. I could not get the taste of grease, blood, cum and my own shit out no matter what I did. I showered, but I couldn't wash away the smell. And then I noticed the bite marks on my own dick. They were deep. They hurt. I didn't even remember that.

I had kept $20,000 in the room to get home, but it was gone. So was my phone, but my wallet was there, and in it my debit card. I had $22,000 in that account, so that should get me to Galveston and let me do what I needed to do. I grabbed a bottle of vodka from the mini bar and shot it down whole. I basically cleaned out the whole bar. Even the glow it created could not erase the stench or take away the pain in my back, legs and ass. And my throat. And my dick. All I knew was I was never going back to Boudreaux's boat, no matter what happened next. I slept for a while, booked a flight and got to the airport. I got kicked out of the bar for ordering half a bottle of jack in about 15 minutes. "You wan' die boy?" The bartender said in his Cajun accent. I only heard Boudreaux. Roughly 30 hours later, I walked into my condo in Galveston. Everything was there as I had asked. My ass was bleeding again, and I knew I needed a doctor. But if I did everything right, it wouldn't matter.

BOOK 19: THE GOSPEL ACCORDING TO LOUIS CHAPTER 12

Bottle's almost empty. So this is where we started. My name is Louis. I killed Jesus. And my friend Michael. All because I was a fucking cynical coward. I don't know what happened to Jesse. Once I was taken to the cabin, I saw nothing else until I woke up in the room. But he was close to dead when I went in there. So I wish I had the words for you. I'm extremely drunk at this point. Was Jesse Jesus? Yeah, I think so. Which means I have to live with...but you already know that.

Sure, he could have just been a con man. But that's not for me to decide anymore. My role here is done. I told the story. I included Mare's and Michael's works. I left them just the way they did them. I did not realize how much they really liked me. How much they had me pegged. Michael. The worst of us. And the best. Mare, who became our leader. I know everyone will hate me now. And I'm sorry about that, especially to Sophie. But there is no way I can live after this. Even if he wasn't Jesus, even if it wasn't my fault, it's not that. It's that memory of Boudreaux and the boat I can't live with. The stink of fish and diesel and Boudreaux's sweaty greasy dick. I can never wash it all away. It's been three days, and it seems like moments ago. I would have been scared to kill myself. After Boudreaux? It will be easy. It's funny, the DDs -- they all found redemption. For me, it's too late. Me, who had already been living his life outside the cave. I had everything I wanted. I didn't need redemption. And now the one person who could give it to me is gone. Because of me. Well played, dip shit.

I see some SUVs coming this way. I guess that's Michael's people. I would tell them the truth, but if they take the time to read this, they will learn it themselves. I have to remember to hit the print button before I kill myself so they have a hard copy. They might not notice the disc. Fuck, that would suck. I should have thought all of this out better. Fuck it. It's time for me to checkout. It's funny. I look at this and think maybe I am a shit writer. Look how long my fucking suicide note is. I'm sorry, Jen. I should have texted you. I couldn't after what happened. I hope you read this. Of course, I hope you edit it, too, and make it much better. I think Sophie would have been OK and moved on. I would have wanted to be part of the kid's life, but I think it would have been you, Jen. Fuck, if not for that boat...I don't know. I really don't. It doesn't matter anymore. I loved you. Sophie too. Shit, maybe you don't want to hear that.

I can almost hear you editing this. "I want pristine copy, Louis. Sober up and try again. More development of the other characters. I am interested in this dentist. In Pete. Give me more of them." But honey, I could not write this sober. I had to be drunk. And high. Killed the last of the Vancouver weed. No way I was going to let that go to waste. I'm sorry I did not do a better job. But that's the story. I'm crying now. One last swig. Never leave alcohol on the table. And now it's time. Do what I said I was going to do at the very beginning. Take the coward's way out. The barrel feels cold against my head. I wonder how long it will take before I am gone? Just the flash and darkness? Shit, I think I already asked that. I really am pretty fucked up now. I would have to be. Jesus, my ass hurts. Well, I hear doors closing outside. It's time. I have one more thing to say and then I am pulling the trigger.

I didn't want money. Fame. Love, I wanted one thing in life, and I know I failed. Fucking sucks, man. I wanted to be a great writer. At least I remembered to push the print button.

BOOK 20: THE GOSPEL ACCORDING TO ANONYMOUS, CHAPTER ONE

I can't tell you how I came to be in possession of this story, or what my name really is. This was written under a pen name and the disc was given to me under a confidentiality agreement. I was only able to read it because I signed the agreement and accepted those terms. So that part of the story must remain a mystery. I also am not really comfortable calling this a "gospel," but that's how the original writer labeled these, and I felt it was a moral imperative to adhere to his style.

The first 19 chapters are exactly as they were written or transcribed by a man named Louis Cravens. He was found dead with a single gunshot wound to the head in a condo in Galveston in May, 2009. Police found no traces of a suicide note or a computer. There was only an empty bottle of Jack Daniels and a Glock model G37, determined to be the method of suicide. Cravens was a journalist who spent his final years writing feature stories for Southwest Monthly, a high end magazine with a subscription base of nearly 40,000. The owner, Marvin Toles, said in a statement that Cravens was "a troubled but terrific talent who never missed a deadline and always found compelling stories of great importance to the community. It is a shame whatever demons he had claimed his life. He will never know the impact he had."

An autopsy revealed signs of significant recent sexual abuse. The coroner said Cravens had been right – he actually died on that boat. The damage was so significant; even medical care would have likely been too late. He was surprised Cravens lasted as long as he did and managed to make it to Galveston. Internal bleeding, permanent damage to numerous internal organs…whoever abused Cravens had done enough damage to kill him.

What happened after Cravens pulled the trigger is mostly conjecture, but there were interviews conducted with people who claim to have been at the scene. Unfortunately, they, too, must remain anonymous. I agreed to those terms so you would know what happened. As Cravens was ending his life, the man likely referred to as Frankie V. and several of his associates pulled up to the condo. When they heard the shot, they immediately burst in. I'm told Frankie looked old and tired. He spoke to Louis' dead body, telling him, "You got off easy, you son of a bitch. I wanted your ass alive. I wanted to know what really happened. Not buying Rossi's bullshit on this. No way Scraps went out like that." His men spread around, checking to see if anyone heard the shot. If so, the police were coming. But apparently no one had.

Frankie's men found the computer, along with pages that were still printing out. Frankie took a particular interest in what happened when the three men left the hotel for a golf game that would never happen. "OK, boys, take all the written stuff and the laptop. Clean up everything that looks like we were here. And let's get the fuck out of here."

"What are we going to do with his story?" an associate asked.

"Read it. Maybe it will tell us what happened to Scraps." Frankie lit up a cigarette, and quietly walked outside. He stared at the sky, trying to decide what to do next. "It looks like an entire book, boss," the associate said. "Take the whole thing. If it's good, I know a kid who can make it better. This guy doesn't need it anymore." As Frankie finished his cigarette, a siren could be heard in the distance. Someone had called the police after all. But Frankie and his crew would be long gone by then. The siren is briefly drowned out by the loud engine of a Harley, riding past on a lonely road. No one got a good look at the rider, but he appeared to have long hair.

BOOK 21: THE GOSPEL ACCORDING TO ANONYMOUS CHAPTER TWO

I believe this disc was Louis Cravens' suicide note. Again, I apologize for the mystery as to how it came to be in my hands, but it can't be helped. I've published a few things, and my source thought I would know what to do with it. I don't know how much is actually factual, but there is proof of many of the characters and stories did happen. And the growth of the Jessian Religion is a matter of public knowledge.

My contribution is merely to tell you what happened to some of the people Cravens mentioned, share as many facts as possible, and let you decide how much is accurate. I am not a member of the Jessian faith, or in fact a believer in anything. The man known as Michael "Scraps" DiPoto was most certainly Anthony Danario, who lived in New York for several years. His brother Michael died when they were children. Danario owned vending businesses in New York and Houston, and was never implicated in any crimes. He was allegedly shot in an incident outside a New Orleans casino in a robbery attempt and was well known to frequent Sam Houston Race Park under the name "Michael." The man referred to as Frankie V. would almost have certainly been Francis Capriati, a businessman with ties to New York, New Orleans, Galveston and Houston. Capriati has never been implicated in any crimes, either. He is the founder of the popular "Stanley's" restaurant chains. When asked if he was the Frankie V. in the story, Mr. Capriati denied all knowledge and threatened to sue if mentioned by name. He did attend the same high school as Danario, where they starred in the same backfield. Danario played fullback, lettered twice and wore No. 31. Capriati passed away of natural causes late last year, which prompted the release of this book. He was survived by his wife, Kerry Siemens, an attorney who now runs his businesses, and their two-year-old daughter Meg, as well as a son from a prior marriage. His son has a PHD in Creative Writing from Houston and is now a professor at the school. He has published several critically acclaimed works, including two books of poetry, and his historical novel on the Galveston Mafia is being made into a movie.

Jonathan Rossi indeed ran the Silverthorn Casino in New Orleans. He was killed in a car accident along with several of his associates two weeks after Cravens' death. No evidence of foul play was found. The SUV they were driving in collided with a dump truck and crashed into the Mississippi River. No one in the SUV survived the crash. The dump truck driver's body was never recovered.

As for Jesse Christian, there is no physical proof of his existence. The only people who claim to have seen him at the racetrack are members of the Jessians. No one outside the religion has confirmed any sightings. There are no records of a driver's license, social security number or birth certificate for a Jesse Christian who fits the age range described in Cravens' work. Ronald Stanton, an oil rig worker from Lake Charles, La., claimed to have seen a man crucified on a shrimp boat while being flown to his rig by helicopter. The sighting happened at the time

Christian and Cravens would have disappeared from the Silverthorn Casino. Two other passengers agreed they saw "something odd" but could not confirm it was a person. Stanton does not profess to believe in the Jessian faith.

There have been many sightings of a mysterious biker believed to be Christian -- all by Jessians -- at events surrounding the church and occasionally at underground poker rooms. The religion believes he will reveal himself again when the time is right. No photos or video exist, either. Sophie Danilo has a photo of herself with Cravens that shows the back of a woman and man with long hair sitting at a bar behind them. Danilo insists this is Christian and Mare Collins and showed me the photo. She added that Christian -- if he did exist -- was adamantly opposed to photos of any kind and that the one she had happened purely by accident. Some have speculated that he was a fugitive going under an assumed name and did not wish to be found out. This theory makes sense in terms of the lack of legal documents and tax filings.

As for the DDs, all of the names checked out and are high priestesses or priests in the Jessian Church. They also were frequent gamblers for many years. IRS records show that the group collected in excess of $26 million in reportable winning tickets over a 14-month span in 2008-09. Most of the IRS tickets were significant scores on pick sixes, pick fives and superfectas. The records do not reveal how much was actually invested. The tickets were cashed primarily by three men -- Pete Thornton, an oil and gas consultant, and Paul Solander, Jr., an attorney with the Solander law firm. Later, several tickets connected to the group were cashed by an Antonio Stasi, including all of the tickets from the 2009 Derby. All members filed income taxes on the winnings. There were no filings under the name Jesse Christian.

Betting consortiums are not uncommon, nor are winnings reaching those totals. The net payoff was likely considerably much less, as syndicates tend to invest significant dollars. Mine That Bird, one of the biggest long shots in Kentucky Derby history, did win the 2009 race and many of the winning tickets on the biggest wagers were cashed at Sam Houston Race Park.

All of the DDs were interviewed and confirmed the numbers, and also said they used the winnings to found the church and grow its message. They insist Jesse Christian was real, and the Jessian church now has a presence in 26 states and a membership of nearly 100,000 and growing. Their fundamental message of redemption, Gnostic values and a belief that all humans are connected regardless of faith has resonated with many throughout America. James Monroe, a former truck driver -- the James referred to by Cravens -- is high priest and the religion's most fervent believer. He runs the flagship church in Houston. He confirmed that everything written about him by Cravens was true, but he admitted he was not there for all of the stories.

The others were each given copies of the manuscript and asked to confirm the stories. All of them did. Mary Madelaine "Mare" Collins is the religion's most revered priestess, operating out of Shreveport, Louisiana and hosts a popular weekly television show on several cable networks. Her daughter, Jessie, fits the age range from the time the DDs were frequenting the race track. In addition to confirming Cravens work, she also confirmed that she had written some of it for Cravens and agreed to let him tell the story.

Sophie Danilo has a son, Louis Cravens Jr. Like the others, she is deeply involved in the church. She insisted the child was Cravens' in her interview. She runs a church in Aspen, Colorado, where she lives with her husband Mark and their two children. They reunited shortly before Louis Jr. was born. Louis Jr. is the same age as Collins' daughter.

All 12 have given up all or most other business interests to grow the faith except Jim Caldwell, who runs a church near his catfish farm -- which he still operates -- in Beaumont, Texas. Alan Silver heads up the Dallas church, the second largest in America. Bilal and Sonia Bahawalanzai are based in Destin, Florida. Paul Solander Sr. and Jr. turned their law firm over to a new partner and started churches in Los Angeles and San Francisco, respectively. The firm is still profitable and they retained ownership and still collect checks. Both men are extremely wealthy.

Pete Thornton is in Louisville, Kentucky. Bernie Moscowitz no longer practices dentistry and started the church in New York City. All except Sophie continue to frequent race tracks and casinos. She says she hasn't gambled since the weekend in New Orleans and no longer has any desire to do so. As of this writing, she was pregnant with her fourth child, her third with her husband Mark. She insists they are happier than they have ever been. They all confirm everything Cravens wrote was the truth, and he is considered a tragic hero in the faith, a man who had to be sacrificed for the message to grow. They believe the release of his work will expand the faith considerably, which is why I suspect they were all so cooperative with my end of this. They do seem to believe deeply in their religion, and the fundamental message is indeed appealing. They do not appear to be the typical evangelical scam artists, but that's also what good con men and women do, and racetracks are filled with them. It's entirely possible that's all this is, and that the man they called Jesse Christian was the best con man of all.

The interviews they provided would be enough to fill another book. I simply used them for background and confirmation here, so as to not detract from Cravens' story, and allow you to draw your own conclusions. I did seek out two people not associated with the faith in hopes of getting information not tainted by their beliefs. One was a former co-worker of Cravens', Gennara "Jennifer" (Jen) Haddad. She declined to be interviewed in depth for the record, but did admit to an on-again, off-again romantic relationship with Cravens. She lives in a downtown Houston penthouse with her twins, Louis and Mala Haddad, and their nanny. She does part time editing now, and admits she inherited a significant amount of money, but won't say from where. She was cooperative, but also admitted she was working on her own book on her relationship with Cravens over the years, and did not wish to share that information until her book comes out. She says the Louis Cravens she knew is much different than the one who wrote this book. She believes alcohol slowly destroyed him. She did confirm the twins were Cravens' children.

In addition, she did share some fascinating stories off the record, which she will include in her own book. I look forward to reading it. She is much like Cravens described her. Beautiful, funny, smart, a terrific editor, and from what I could tell, a great mom. I have enjoyed spending time with her and getting to know her. As for Boudreaux, our research found dozens of men fitting that description working shrimp boats in Louisiana. We could not realistically pinpoint anyone who might have been the person referred to in the book. And the name Boudreaux in Louisiana is like Smith anywhere else. But it's not hard to assume he exists, especially considering the substantial physical damage done to Cravens, and the fact that most of his other stories checked out. The Boudreaux of the book obviously is not someone who wants to be found.

So what does it all mean? Was Jesse Christian really the Jesus of his time? A race track con man? A dream creation designed to create a new religion? Was Louis Cravens really Judas? Or just a troubled, drug-ridden alcoholic driven to suicide by an unspeakable rape and depression over the death of his friend Michael? Did his roller coaster of emotions finally lead him to kill himself? Was it fear of the man they called Frankie V.? Sadly, his story has created significantly more questions than answers. After all my research, I have come up with some conclusions of my own.

In reality, Jesse Christian is likely a myth. Every religion needs an origin story, and the dramatic growth of the Jessians, a religion founded by a group of gamblers who financed their faith through winning tickets -- fits the profile of every other religious origin story. A savior who transcends humanity and his or her followers and has to die for the faith to be born. It's an old tale, one we have heard many times before. The only thing that doesn't add up is why Cravens would create such a myth, one that so many people have embraced. There are enough facts to lend credence to much of the story. Certainly a great deal of it happened as written. But why fictionalize Jesse Christian if everything else appears to be true? I also initially wondered why he would kill himself, but the details on the boat might drive anyone to that result. It's also possible he knew his injuries were mortal and took his life before they did. I believe the sexual assault is the real reason he killed himself.

It's also entirely believable he married fact to fiction in order to help his friends launch a new religion. It's also possible the facts and fiction became blurred through Cravens' significant use of drugs and alcohol. As many questions seem to surround Cravens as they do Christian. I posed this theory to many of the Jessians: That Jesse and Louis were the same person, in a Tyler Durden, *Fight Club* type of way. They insist that is not the case. And in all honesty, I would find that a bit easy. But the story leaves so much in doubt, so many vagaries. But isn't that what all religion does? Jesse Christian. A prophet, a con man or a talented gambler? Maybe all three? Maybe no one at all?

There is one significant thing I believe the Jessians got right in their beliefs, and it applies to the conclusions we draw from this story: What I believe doesn't matter. What they believe doesn't matter. Ultimately, what you believe matters. And that decision, of course, is up to you.

ACKNOWLEDGEMENTS

This novel has been in the works for a long, long time. I first wrote it in 1995, had a deal to publish, but it all fell apart for a lot of silly reasons. Then it was supposed to be a movie. Then a book again. So the project went into mothballs for a while. When I picked it back up in 2013, I updated the timeline to include the events of Hurricane Ike and its impact on the Gulf Coast. The result is a better story, and hopefully one you enjoyed.

The concept came to me one night while listening to one of my go-to bands, ZZ Top. The song Jesus Just Left Chicago is one of my all-time favorites. In it, Jesus just left Chicago and is on his way to New Orleans. I might have been drinking at the time, but I was listening one night and wondered where he would go in between and decided he would show up at Sam Houston Race Park and make everyone money, and suddenly the idea came together.

I had written several short stories for my Masters Thesis at the University of Houston-Clear Lake in 1989. When I put them together, the themes were all similar -- Houston/Galveston, characters seeking redemption, religion, music, the mafia and of course, gambling. Most of the characters in this novel were born from those stories, as well as a few others I have written over the years. Some were published, but many I just wrote for friends while I was grinding away at an 80-hour a week job at the Houston Chronicle. Michael, for instance, was from a short story called "31," about a hit man who heard music with each kill and associated the two. It was written on an old computer and there were a few printouts for friends, but like most of the others, it is probably lost forever.

So he was reborn in this novel, along with a lot of the other characters. Jesse made appearances in a couple of the earlier stories, and the racetrack theme brought it all together. In the mid-90s, I would spend days at the track with the same table of people, and the concept of the disciples came from there. While none of the characters are based on real life, many of them are compilations of people I have met or stories I have heard.

As far as reality, all of the devastation of Crystal Beach by Hurricane Ike is real, as is Mine That Bird's win in the Kentucky Derby.

You might have noticed the story moves fast. My writing style was born from 20 years in journalism and heavy influences from the late, incomparable Douglas Adams and Elmore Leonard as well as Michael Moorcock, Dick Francis and Stephen King. I have always tried to live by Leonard's words: "Try to leave out the part that the readers tend to skip." I don't do a lot of deep descriptions, instead allowing for the reader to use imagination to fill in the blanks. The exceptions are the poker and horse racing scenes, where hopefully I was able to paint a picture for those of you who do not participate in either.

Discerning readers will notice some inconsistencies and mistakes. Those are by design, as Louis' story was written under a haze of alcohol and weed.

I have several new titles in the works, including a sequel (that's a radio tease). But this story has haunted me and had to be told before I could move on. So now we shall, and look for several new releases soon.

There are too many people to thank, and I don't want to turn this into an Academy Award acceptance speech, so I will do my best to keep it short.

Thanks to the following:

Cris Rodriguez, a former student of mine and a talented filmmaker whose interest in the film version forced me to finish the novel.

Scott Scully, one of my all time favorite gambling partners who will recognize a lot of the characters.

John McClain, who wrote the foreword for this. He is one of my oldest friends and helped keep me almost sane for 20 years at the Houston Chronicle.

Curt Meyer, a brilliant artist who did the cover work for Acing Racing as well as Jesus.

My father, the late Fred B. Faour, the greatest, funniest man who ever lived. An unbelievably talented journalist and an even better friend. The world is a darker place without him. Not a day goes by where I don't think about him.

Jeff Sotman, the best gambler I ever knew and a man who was as close to me as my brothers. We lost Jeff way too young. He was always there and helped me through some bleak times. I wished he had lived to see the final version of this.

Eunice Munoz and Big Fish Marketing. She has always believed in me and promoted me, even when I had serious doubts about myself.

David Gow, CEO of Gow Media, for being a great business partner, boss and friend who has always trusted my ideas for the company (including this) and has supported me through thick and thin.

And my family. My mom, Patricia, who could have been the one writing novels if things had gone a little differently; my grandmother, Lucille, who has kept everything I have ever written and every trophy I ever won; my brothers Patrick and John, who have always been there through every success and failure any of us had.

Of course, my son Will, who is a talented writer in his own right, and my daughter Katie, who vows to be more famous than me (she will be).

My awesome in-laws in Canada, Carl and Lois, who have become like an extra set of parents for me, and accepted me even after their daughter married an American.

And finally, most importantly, my wife Valerie, who has always pushed me, believed in me, but also chopped me down if I got too full of myself. So much of my success has been because she convinced me I could actually do it. I doubt this project would have ever happened without her.

Thanks to all of them, as well as those of you who read this book and for some reason are still reading now. I hope you enjoyed it, and hopefully this is just the beginning.

CPSIA information can be obtained
at www.ICGtesting.com
Printed in the USA
LVHW012056210119
604681LV00019B/804/P